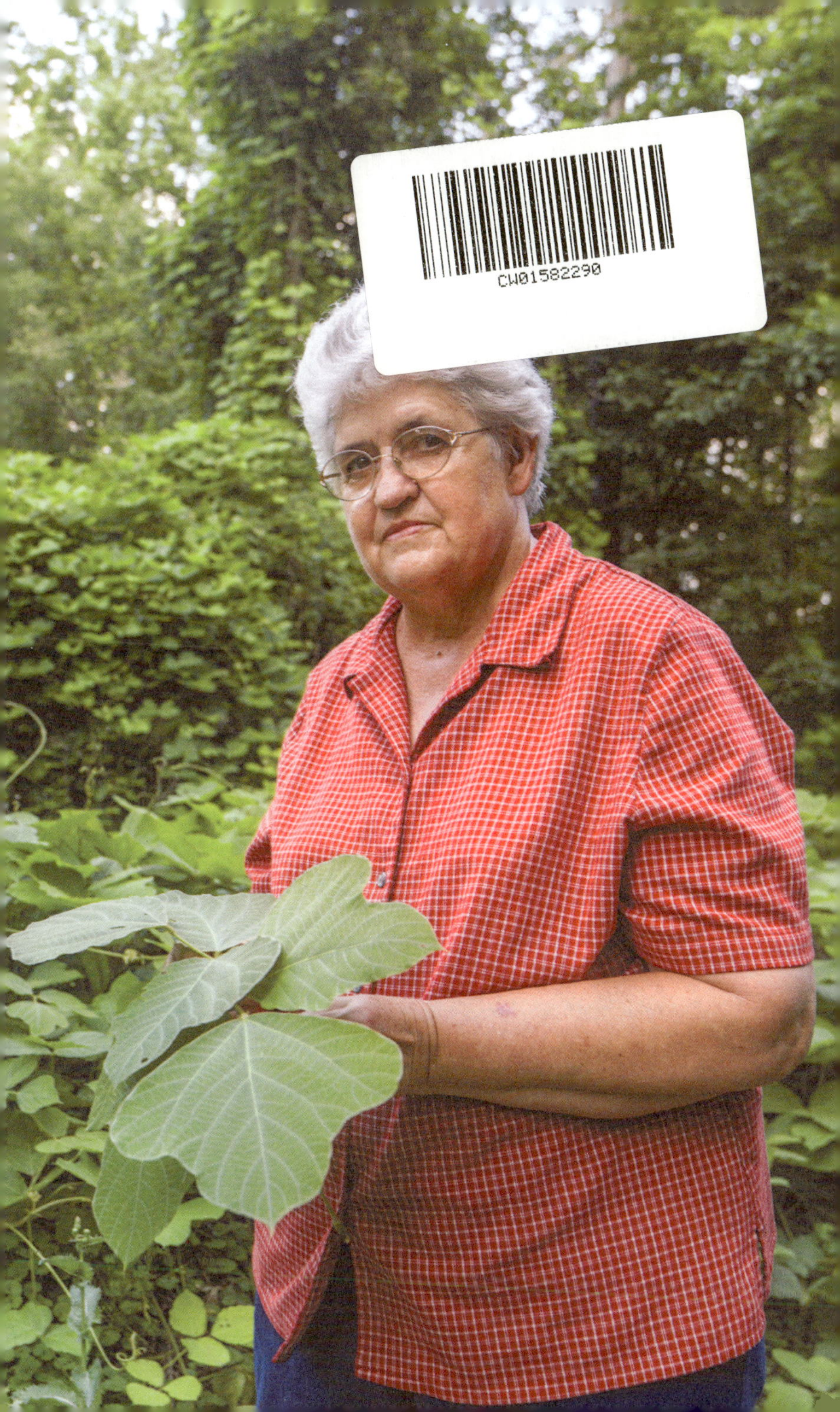

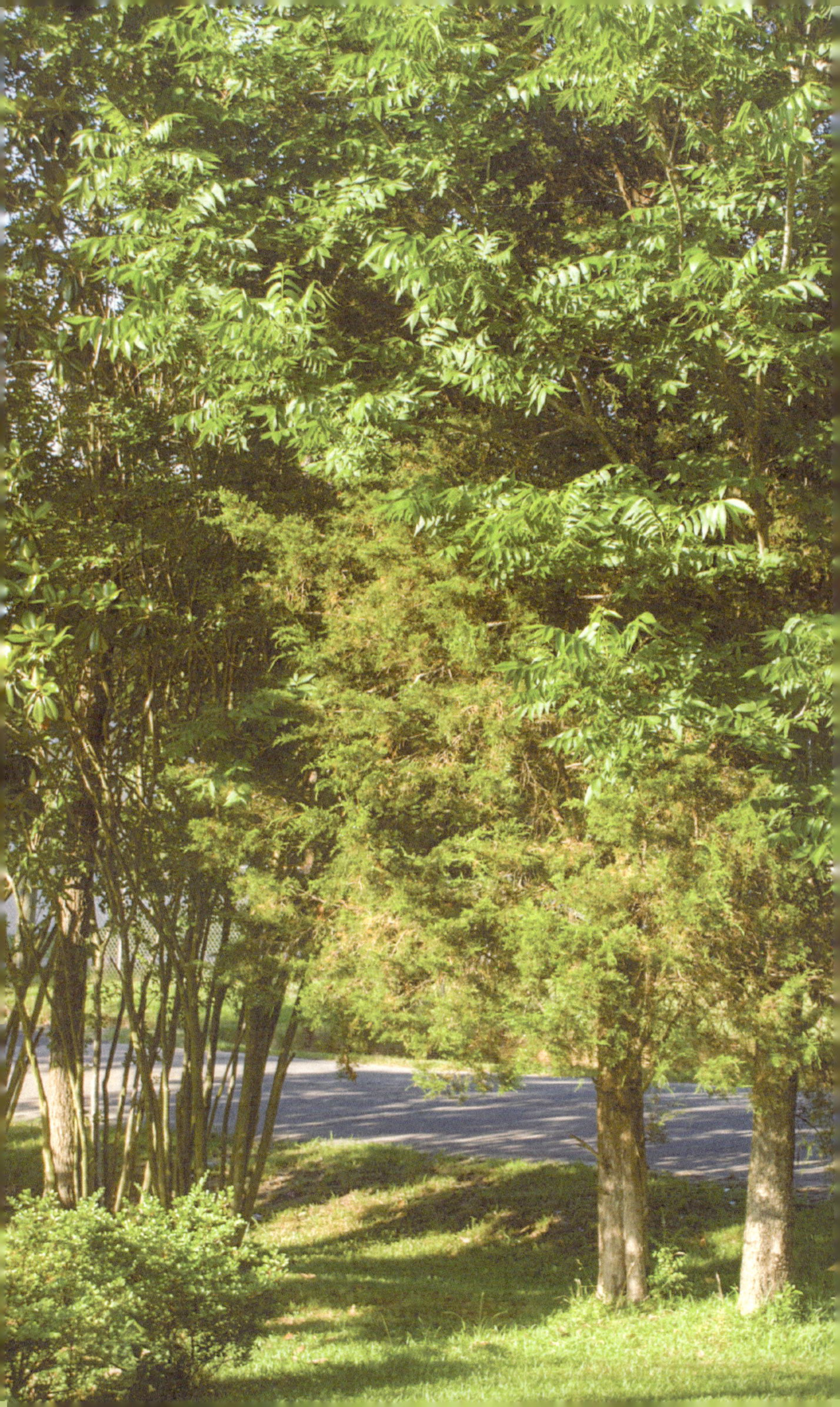

# Making Culture by Hand

## BETTYE KIMBRELL

Photographs and Interviews
by **Alan Govenar**

Published by Documentary Arts, Inc.
www.documentaryarts.org


First Edition



ISBN: 979-8-9915022-4-5

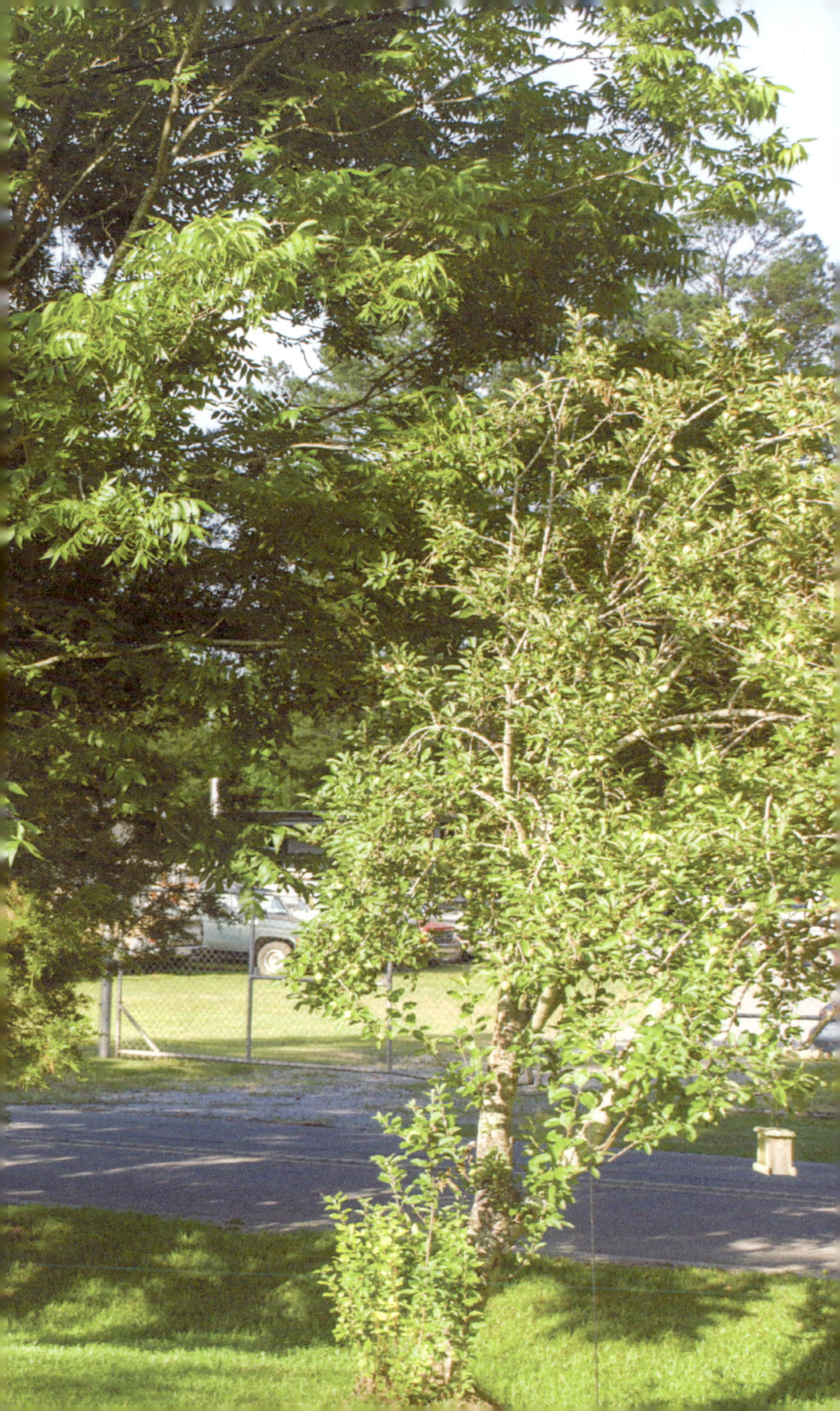

# My Story

My grandmother, Julie Frances Whitson, raised me. I grew up on a farm in Fayette County in central Alabama, about fifty-five miles west where I am now in Jefferson County. Everybody worked. And she thought idle hands were the devil's workshop. So, she was very good at keeping us busy. When we weren't doing farm chores, she had us piecing scraps together by hand to make bed covers. The process of quilting has never changed. It's a layering process; it's stitching the layers together. So, what you actually wind up with depends on what you stitched together and in what fashion.

My father was named Bradley Whitson, and my mother was Pearl Woods Whitson. But she didn't like us, and she walked off and left us. And we suffered some from it, especially during that time period in the late 1930s, early '40s, because we were in a small community, a small town, where everybody is related. And as strange as it might seem in today's world, a neglectful parent was a stigma. We had to live with that stigma of having a mother that didn't love us. It caused some social problems for a while, but I think it made me a better person.

My grandmother made our clothes. She used the leftover fabric from usually some type of feed or fertilizer sacks, or even cut down adult clothes that they no longer wore and made clothes for us. So, the fabric we used in quilts, that was its last life. It couldn't be used for anything else. They were typically called string quilts, and that just meant they were made from the strings of leftover clothing or whatever else we had. String quilts usually are just small strips of fabric that can be anywhere from a quarter of an inch to three or four inches wide.

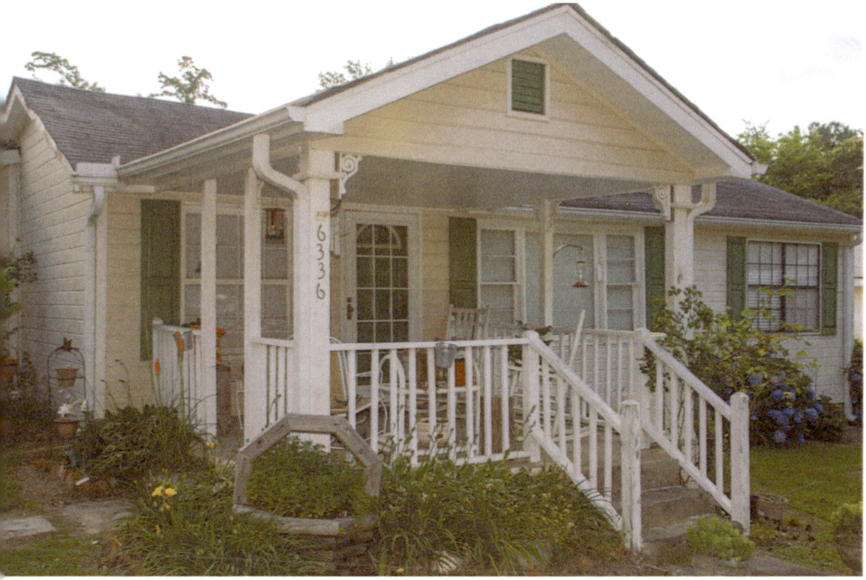
6336

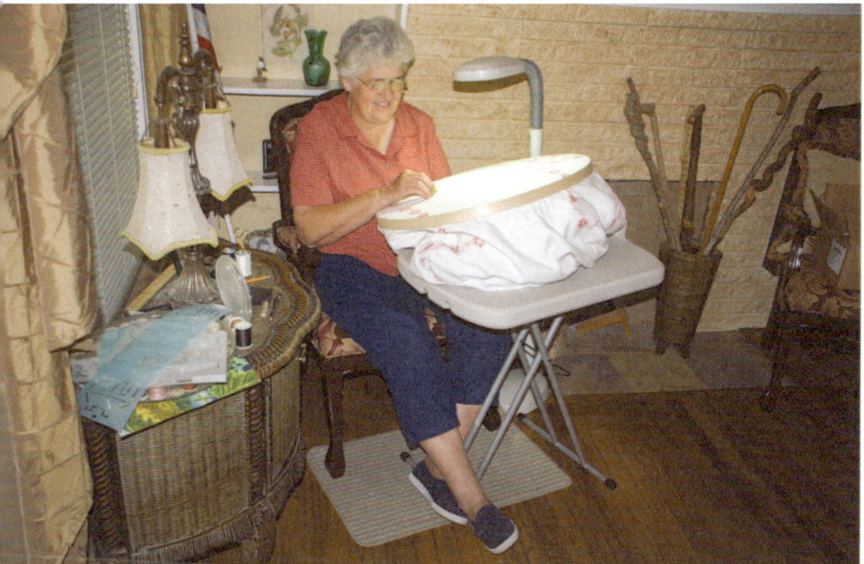

I had a desire to please my grandmother. She was a very strict disciplinarian. She was a person who knew where everything she had was. Everything she did was exact and for a purpose. So, my goal was to be sure that I did exactly what she told me to do. I had a great desire to emulate her, although at the time I didn't know that.

I learned to quilt from my grandmother by her showing us what to do and how to do it, pretty much as we do today. Oh, we had boxes; I'm talking cardboard boxes of strings that would be collected over a period of time. We used the early paper piecing method, where we would sew the strings to the paper and then cut the shape of the paper out and finish piecing the quilt from there. We did it around the fireplace at night, or if it was raining and we couldn't be outside working or doing things like this. It was an ongoing process. There was never a time there wasn't a quilt in process.

My grandparents had a 160-acre farm that they farmed with two mules. I mean, we had corn, cotton, and all the vegetables. And we had our livestock and our farm animals. We had pigs and chickens. We were self-sufficient, pretty much.

I went to school in Berry and Bankston, which was about fifteen miles away from where we lived. We walked two miles to catch the school bus. Now, I know my kids say, "This is going back to the dark ages, Mom, people don't do that anymore." And I tell them, "Thank goodness you don't have to." So, I lived in isolation. I had a person ask me one time, "Did you think you lived in poverty?" Not really because everybody else was in the same situation. Everybody we knew lived like we did. I mean, we actually were poor people, but we didn't know that. So, it didn't bother us.

I remember before Dad and Mother separated, my daddy worked at a lumber yard. He was one of the main people. And he had a lot of black guys that worked with him in the lumberyard. So, I played with black children. I don't think the animosity that happened later in Alabama was there because each one of us respected the other. It was because the black people that lived in rural areas, a lot of them owned their own farm and they wanted the same respect that they gave us. They expected the same respect back.

I made my first quilt when I was ten years old. We worked on this quilt through the summer, my grandmother and my sister and I, and we got two weeks out from school for the Christmas holidays. We put our quilts in an old-fashioned frame, like you see with a group of people sitting around it. Well, my grandmother helped us put the quilt up and the three of us quilted it. That was very difficult to do because the cotton that we used in the quilts was hand carded. It was nothing like the grade of materials that we have to work with now. But I managed to do a good enough job that she approved, and I felt quite proud of myself. It was a string quilt, like Joseph's Coat. It was multicolored.

I didn't start making pattern quilts until the early 1960s. Cindy was my last child, so she was number four at that time. I was a stay-at-home mom and I started getting quilt magazines and saw how they were planned and had a desire to do that. So, I read about what to do, and I'd make mistakes, start over and redo them.

Mostly, I can remember making something like the Dutch Girl pattern, which is pretty much universal. But, there again, I was still using fabric leftover from the girls' dresses and things like that. I bought some fabric, but I used some that I had on hand.

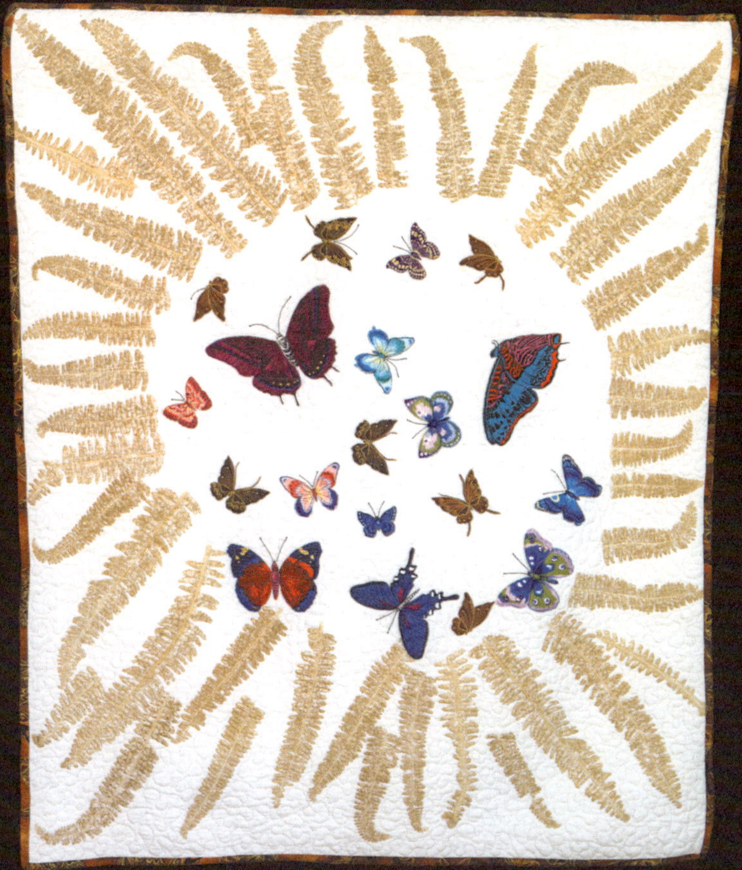

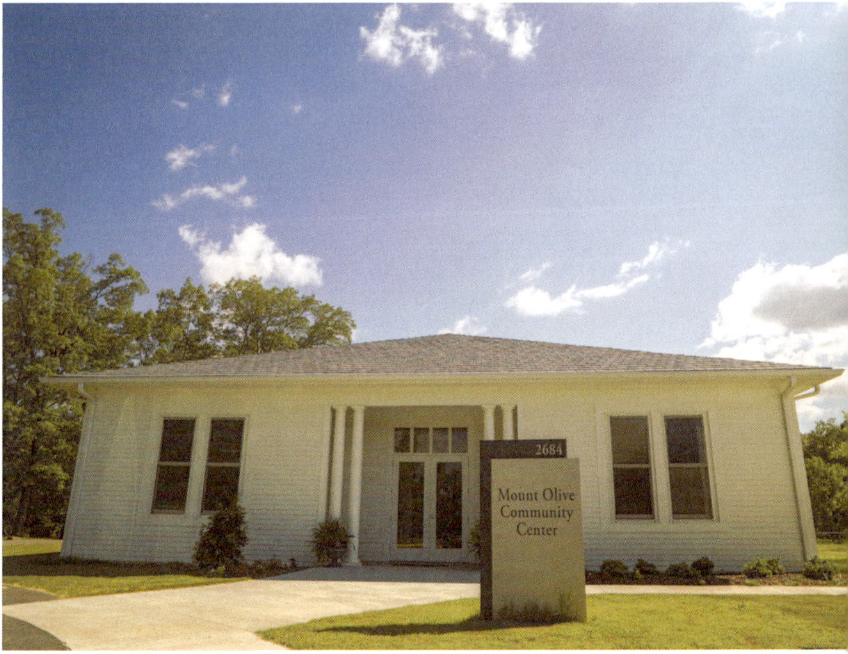


I think we started the North Jefferson Quilt Guild in 1979. Our basic goal has always been that we just share. We get together as a group of ladics. It's the camaraderie, like it's always been in the history of quilt groups, but it'd also about being able to teach other people. I didn't realize there were so many people that didn't' know how. Apparently, quilting missed a couple of generations of people when we became automated and went out and got jobs. So, the Quilt Guild does a good job with mentoring other quilters that come in. If we get a new person in, we try to sit down and talk with them, find out what they like to do, and what they want to make, and then we find a guild member that's going to nurture them through the process. It's kind of, one-on-one, you're getting a special teacher because you're in this group.

Well, if you go back and look at, the church gatherings, and we're talking mule and wagon, pre-automobile, quilting was a very social time for the American woman. And I think it still is. When we get together, we like jabbing at each other and having a real good time, but we also love and pray for each other an awful lot. So, it's a friendship like, it's almost a sisterhood, I guess you could say.

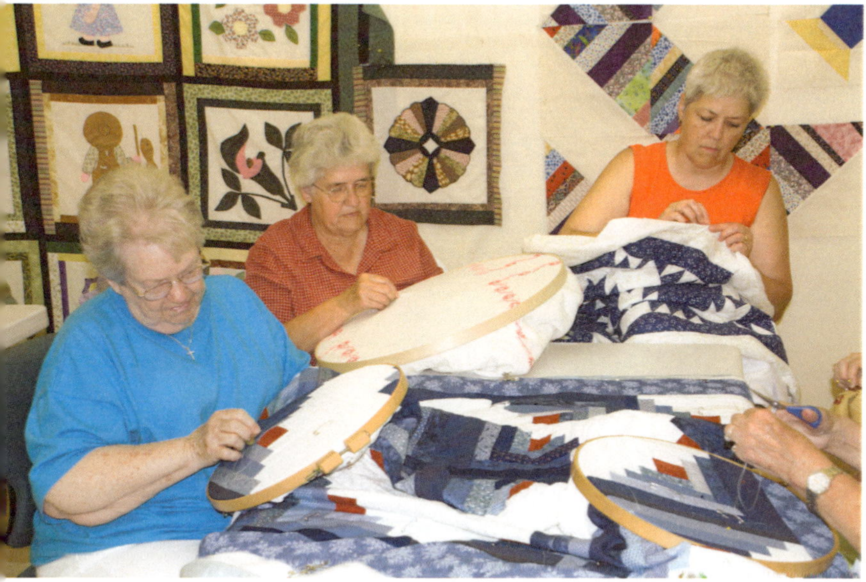

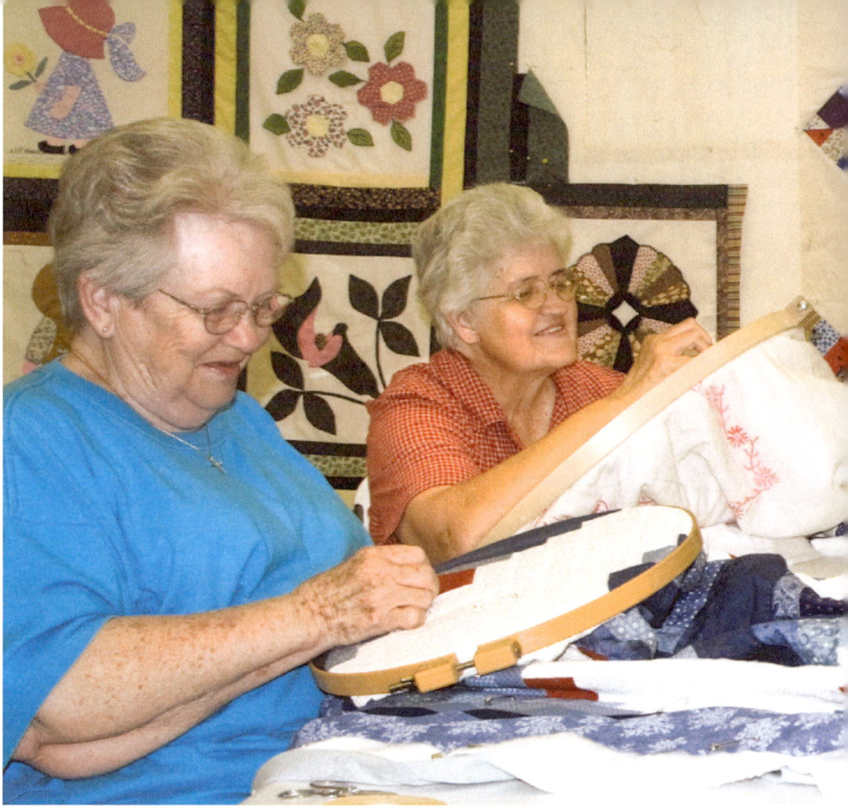

I remember when I still had children at school in Mount Olive, the registrar at the school was a good friend and she was getting near retirement age. And I went by the school one morning and was on my way to quilting, and she said, "Baby, what you…who do y'all talk about when you're at quilt meetings? And I said, "We don't gossip. That's not what we're about." She said, "Oh, come on now. I've been in everything in Mount Olive, church, little league, everything, everybody gossips. I said, "No, unfortunately we just don't have time for that because we're usually working."

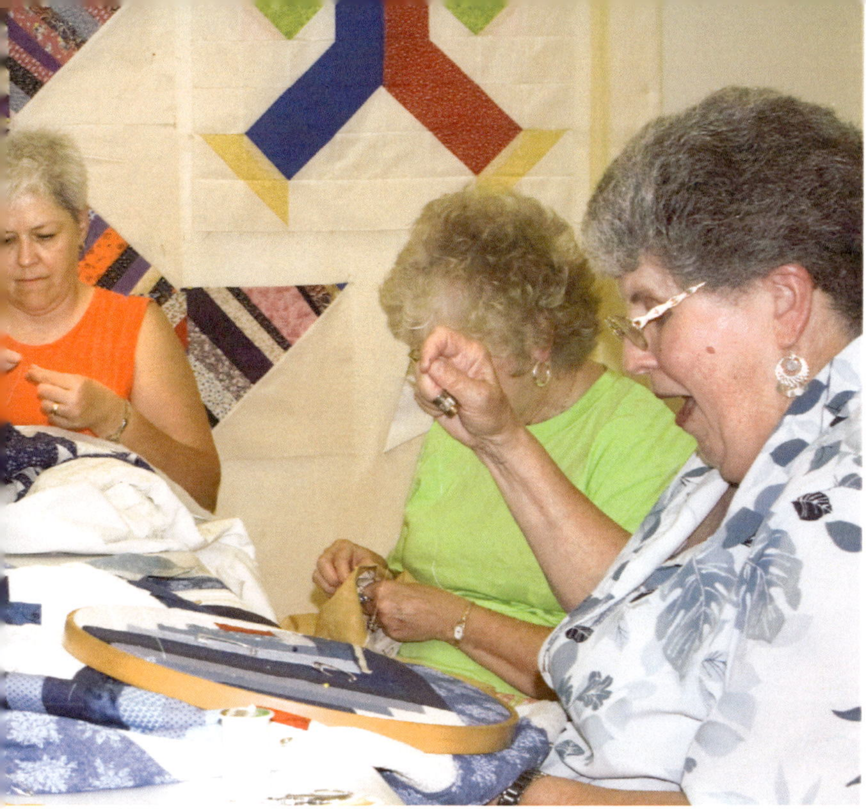

Well, she retired, and two years later, she became a member of the Quilt Guild. And one day she remembered our conversation and she came up to me, she said, “You really don’t gossip. You really are working.” So, I thought that was a real compliment to us, that fact that we had fulfilled her, that she saw that we could actually have a good time and not have to gossip about somebody in the community.

# My Process

I'm still traditional, but I experiment, I push the edge on that experiment. I like anything that's very heavily quilted. I'm a huge fan of the white quilts. I've been fascinated with them for years. The fact is that you can take just a plain piece of fabric, put your needle and thread to it and come out with a wonderful quilt project. They're usually quilted rather heavily, which means they're going to a last a great number of years.

Basically, I use a quilting stitch. But I'm a person who likes to do a lot of heavy quilting. I usually do more than is required. That's the process I enjoy most because by that time, all my design work has been finished and the quilting is usually planned to complement the other elements in the quilt.

Sometimes, we use some of our own designs. Sometimes I use the commercial designs. It's fun to combine the different elements. I tend to mark them with a number two pencil. I find that I have better results. The liquid pens that some of the ladies use now are sometimes absorbed by the batting. Eventually, because it is a chemical, it can come back and eat holes in the quilts. So, there's different ways of getting the transfer designs in. You just have to play with what works best for you.

Putting the quilt together is a three-layering process. It's the same as all other quilts. You have your back, your batting — it's like a peanut butter and jelly sandwich, you have bottom piece of bread, your peanut butter and your jelly, your top, and all that space in between. I quilt in a hoop and then I start having fun.

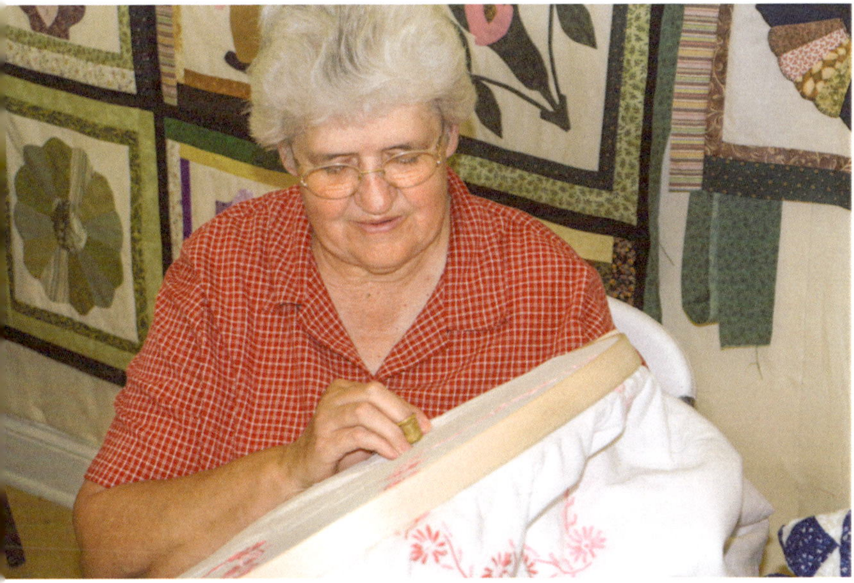

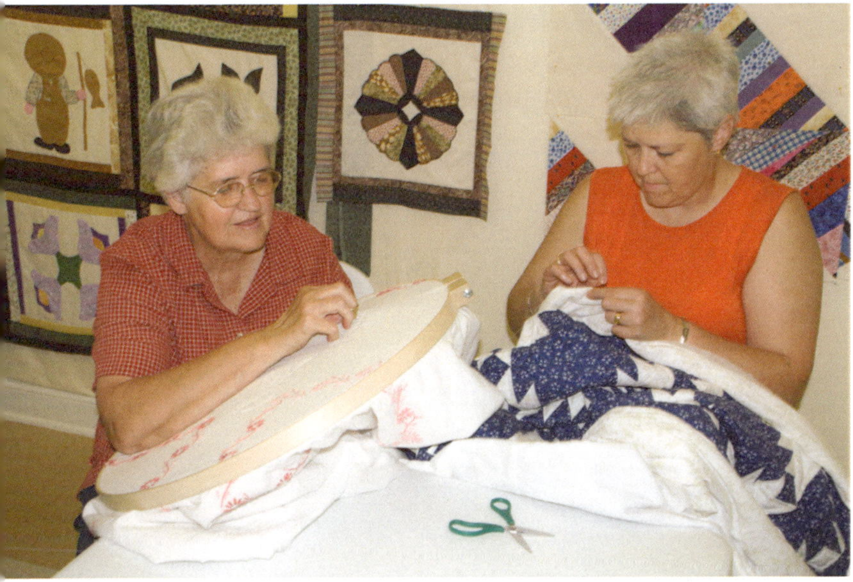

Around 1996, I started leaf pounding plants to make the patterns for my quilts. I had been to a national quilt show in Paducah and saw this lovely little wall hanging that this lady from Alabama, of all places, had made. She had won first place and a $10,000 check, and I thought that was very interesting.

So, I bought a pamphlet with her information in it, and it had a very long list of chemicals in there and I thought I'd never get all these chemicals together. I didn't need them in the house because I had grandchildren in the house. Well, that same week, one of the ladies in the quilt guild came with a spread, it was a typewritten sheet from the University of Alabama, the Museum of Natural History and it talked about Cherokee leaf pounding. And I read it and got very excited because I found out that I could do the leaf pounding and just use vinegar or salt as the mortis, instead of having to use all the chemicals, and I've been leaf pounding the heck out of kudzu and everything else ever since.

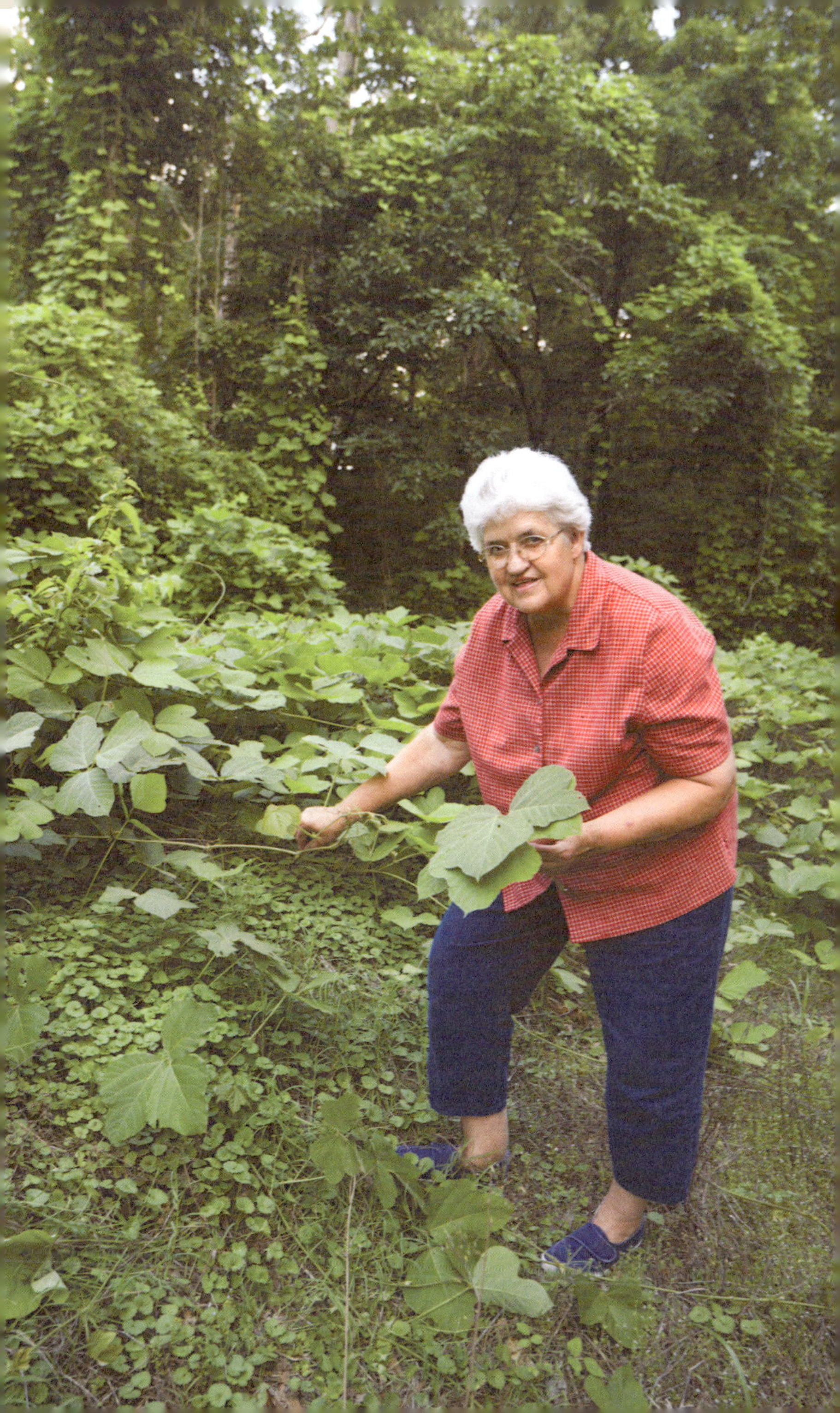

I was on my way to North Carolina, to the John Campbell Folk School to teach a weekend class. So, I tried to go with enough greenery for everybody to have something to pound and see me. And I was headed to Interstate 59, which is a little bit of a turn from where I am.

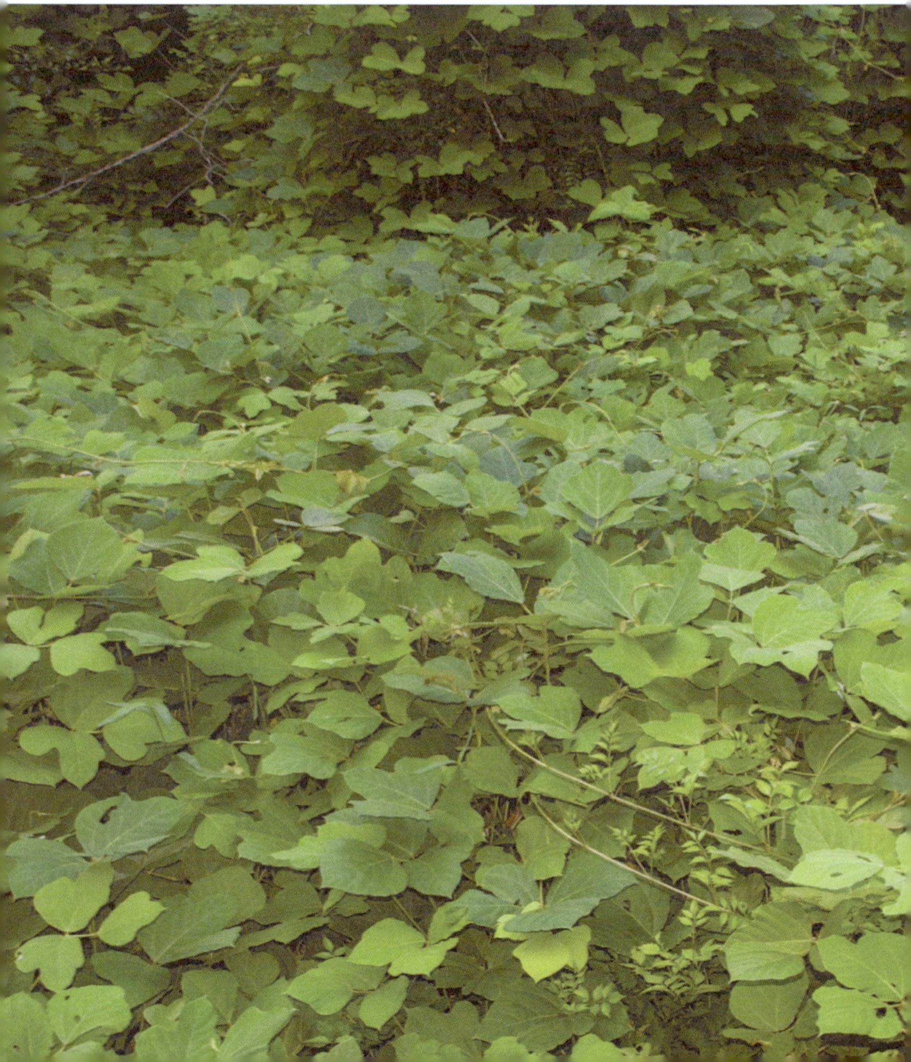

I'm in the Western part of Jefferson County, and 59 is in the Eastern part. So, we had to hit the back roads and go over to I-59, and before we got onto 59, there was a real good kudzu patch alongside the road.

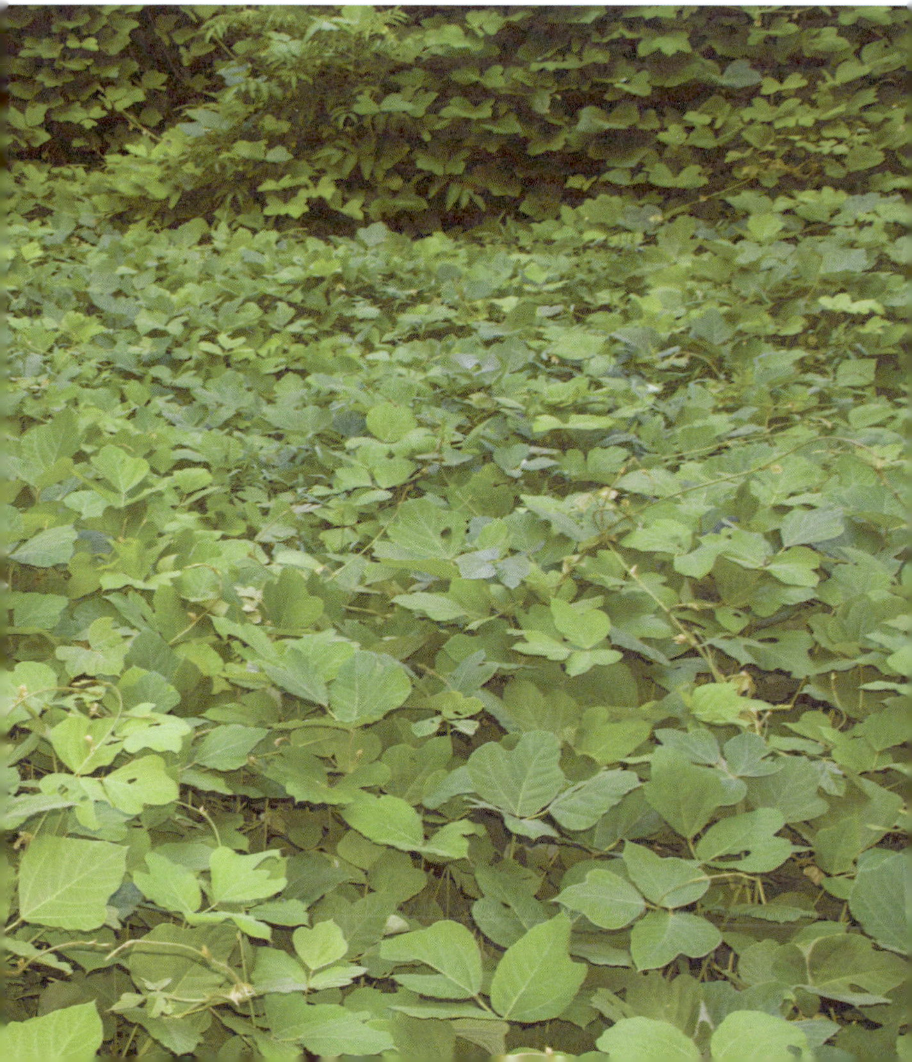

Well, we took a sack with some water in it to gather kudzu, and it started to rain just as we pulled up, and we get out because we knew that was our only chance to get kudzu.

And we started picking kudzu, and everybody driving up and down the road was blowing their horns and waving at us; I'm sure they thought we were fixing to go home and eat turnip greens.

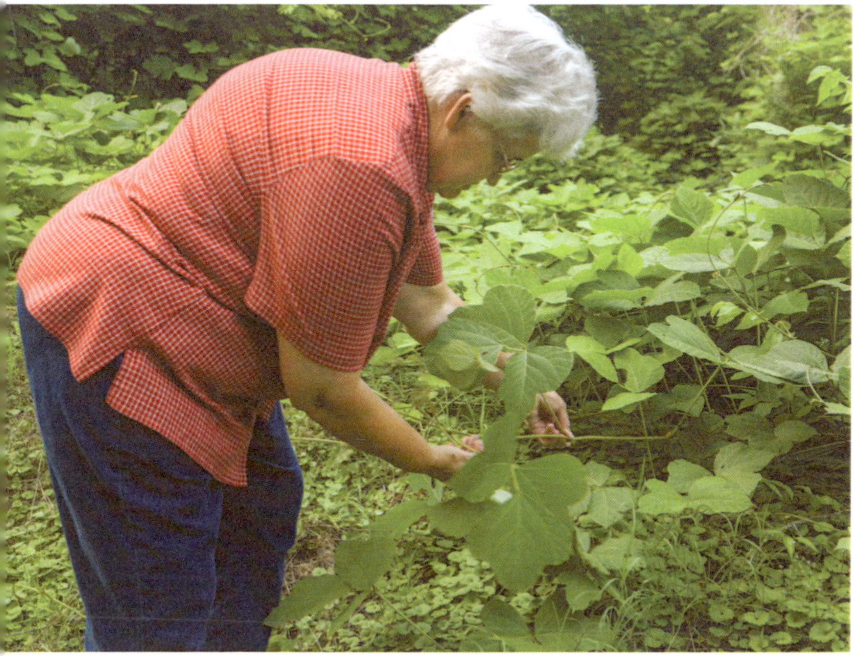

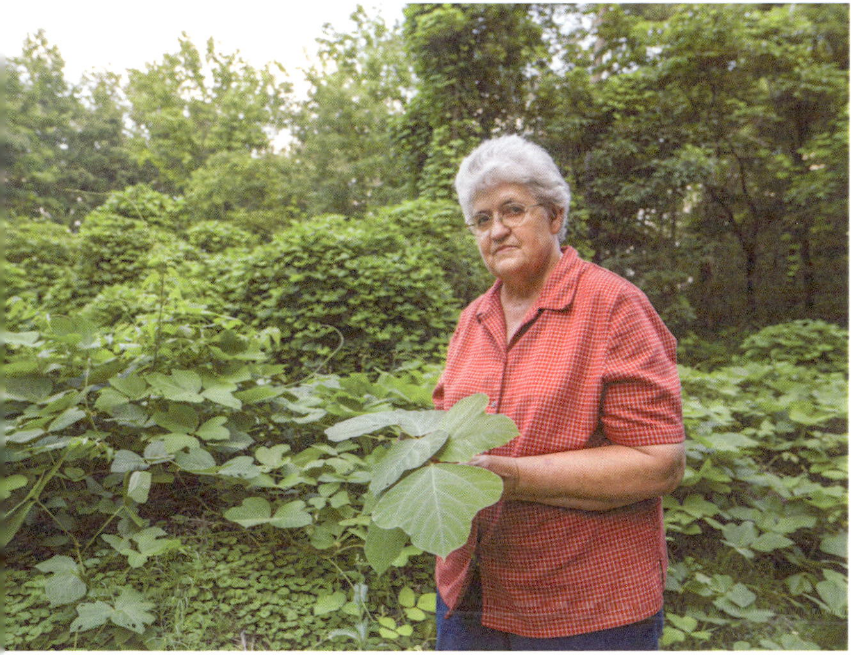

In leaf pounding, the main thing is deciding what I'm going to use. Now, I did do the one with just ferns in it, but I was doing it at a time of the year that we didn't have much greenery here in Alabama and that was the only thing available. I like to be kind of natural. If you look at nature, everything's not straight, all the leaves are not whole, they have bug holes in them. Nature is a mix. It's in every direction. And when I'm doing the leaf-pounded projects, I pretty much liked to do that. I don't organize it, I just find leaves that have an interesting shape or an interesting color and try it and see if it pounds. If it does, it goes into my quilt piece.

The leaf pounding does take a little bit of time. It's not instant gratification.

I mean it, and in some ways, it is because if you tried to manipulate other fabric and get something that looked like a leaf, I believe you'd be more than an hour doing it.

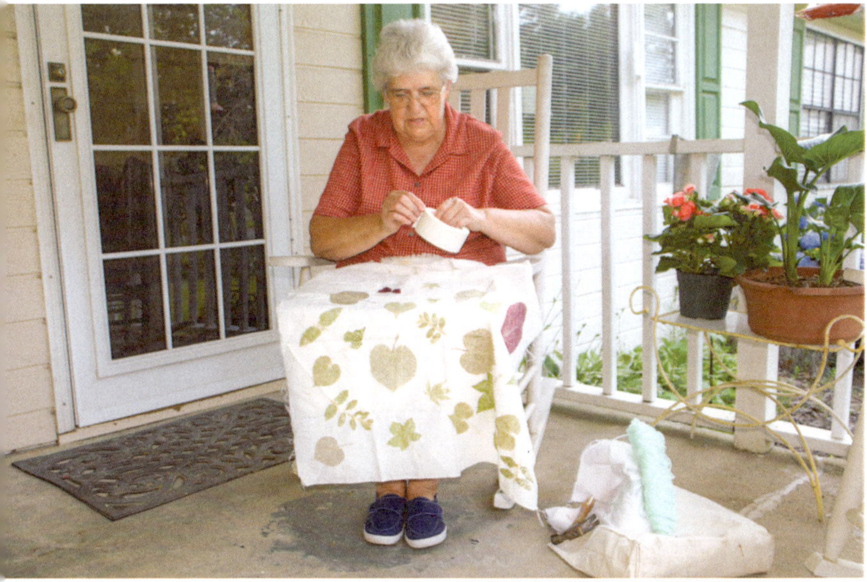

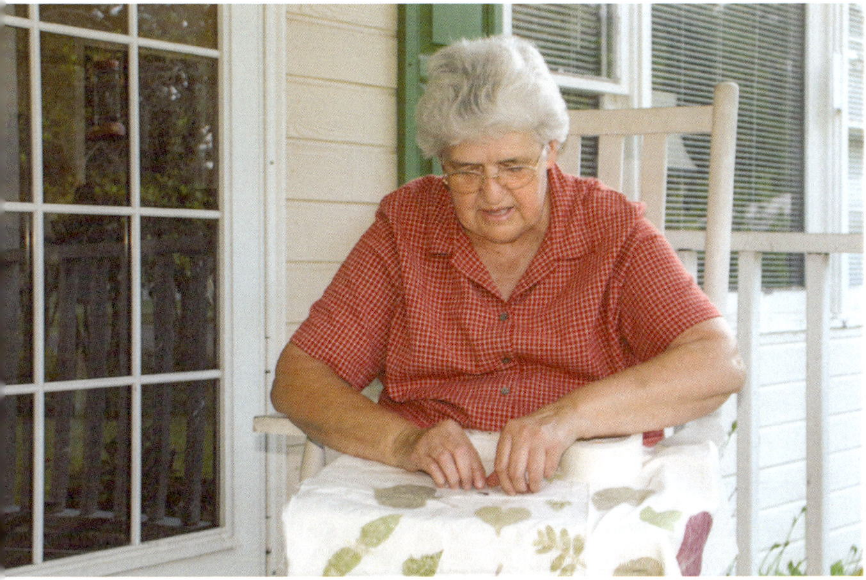

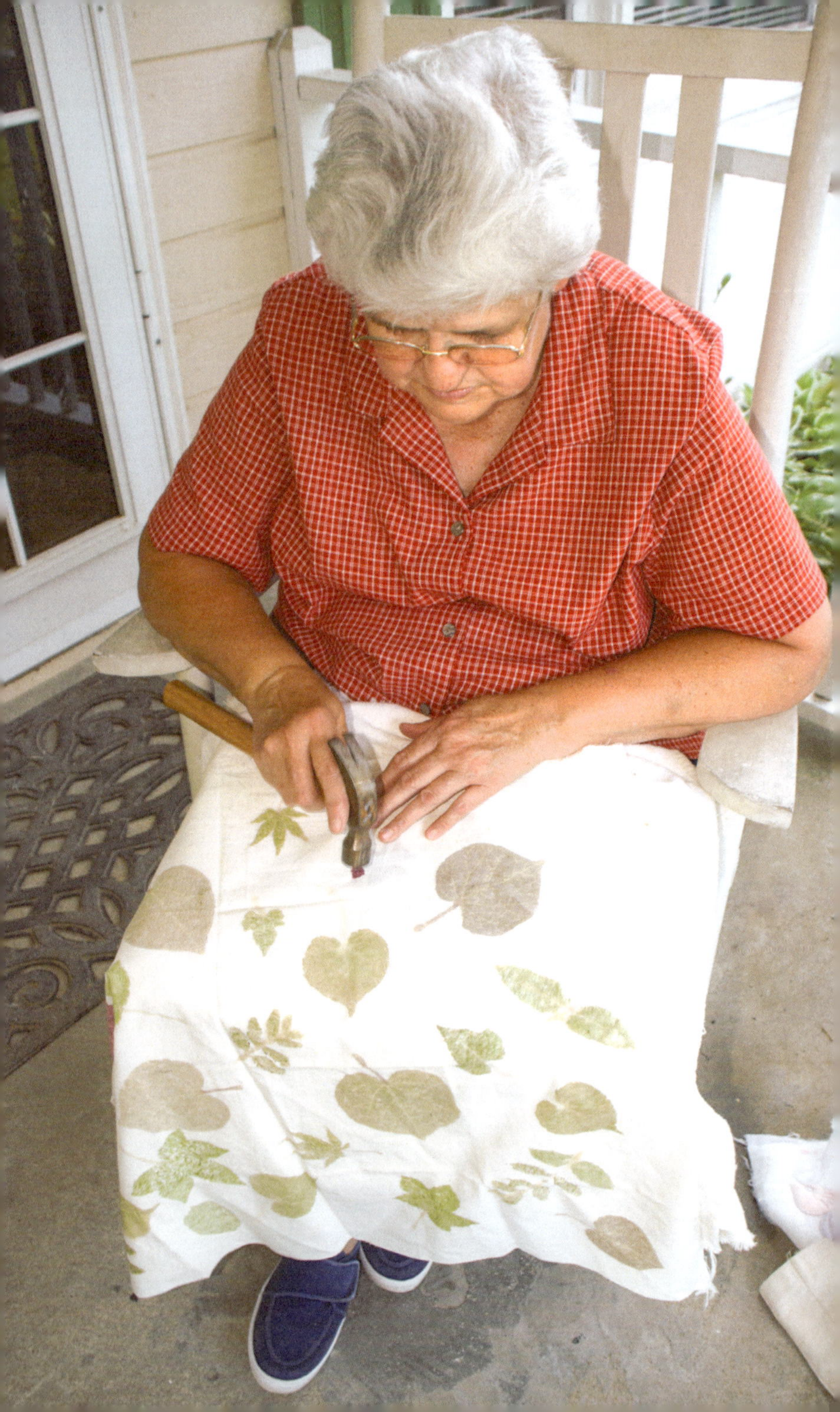

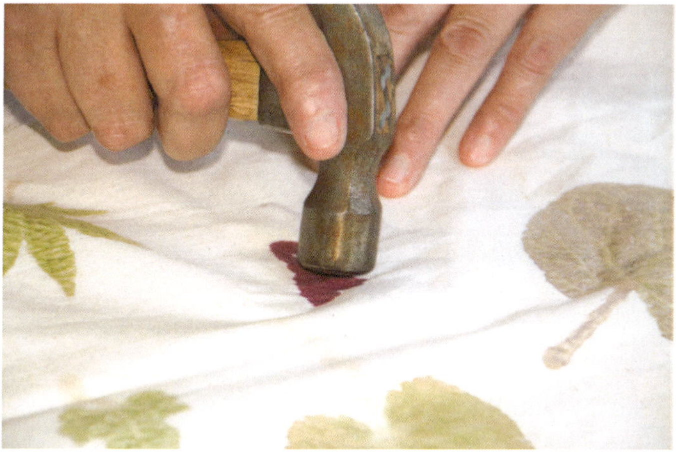

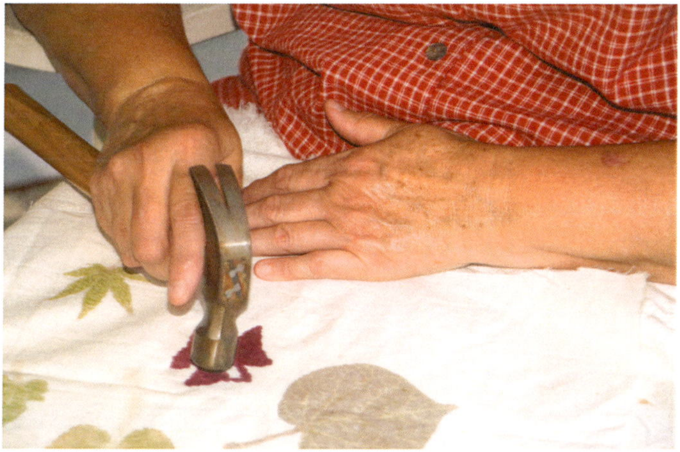

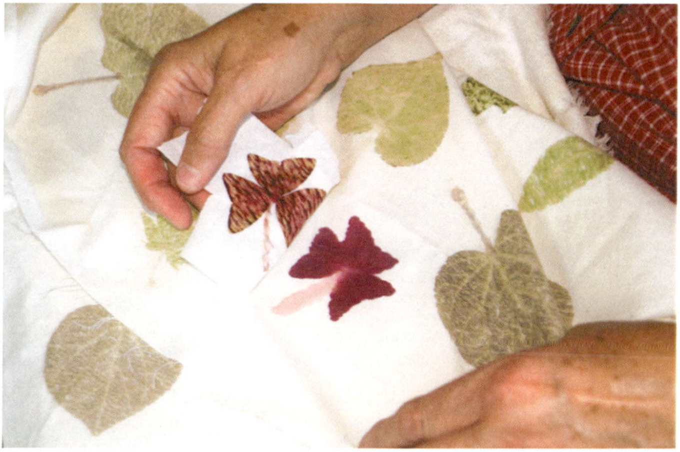

I tape the leaf to the fabric, and here I'm using muslin, which is a cotton fabric, because it's a natural dye, you need to use a natural fiber. I tape the leaf to my fabric, lay it down on a piece of wood, and with the hammer, I gently pound it until I've gotten all the chlorophyll out and the complete shape of the leaf on my fabric.

Now, I can pound on a piece for a year or two, because I might do one leaf today and I might not pick it up again until I go to the country two or three weeks from now. And I see a sassafras leaf that looks really inviting and I'll get it and pound it. The main thing is, before I put it in the quilt process, I've put it in vinegar and water and made that color permanent. Then, I run it through the washer and dryer several times until I'm sure it's not going to bleed.

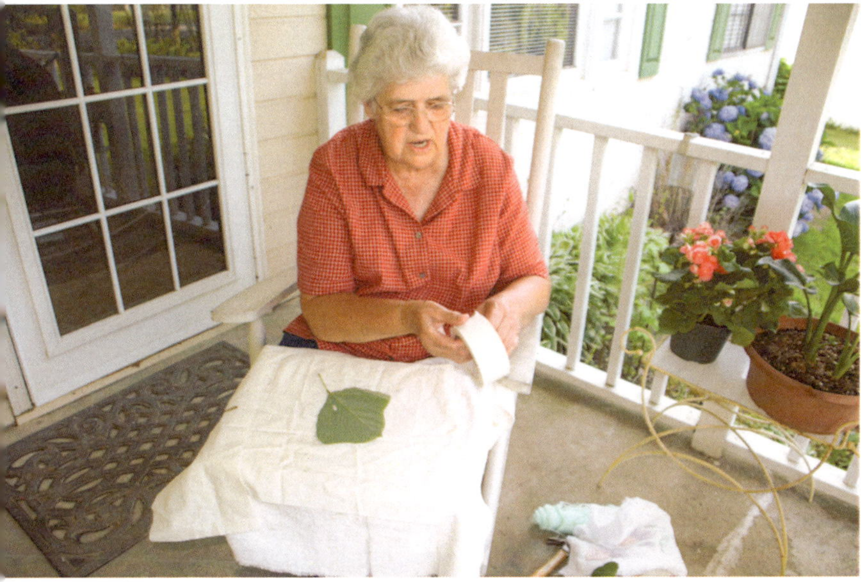

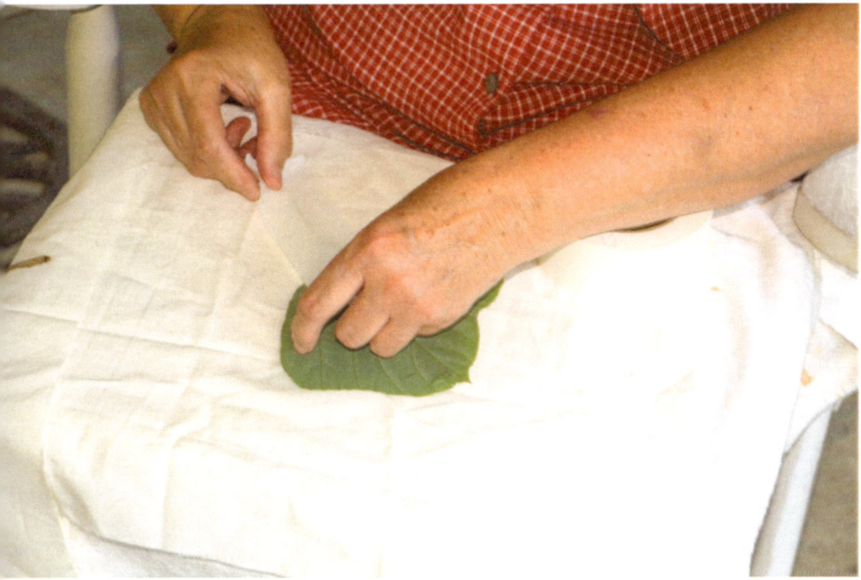

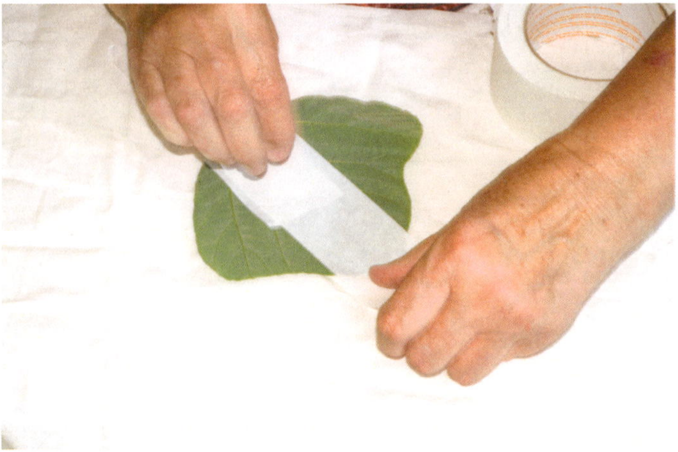

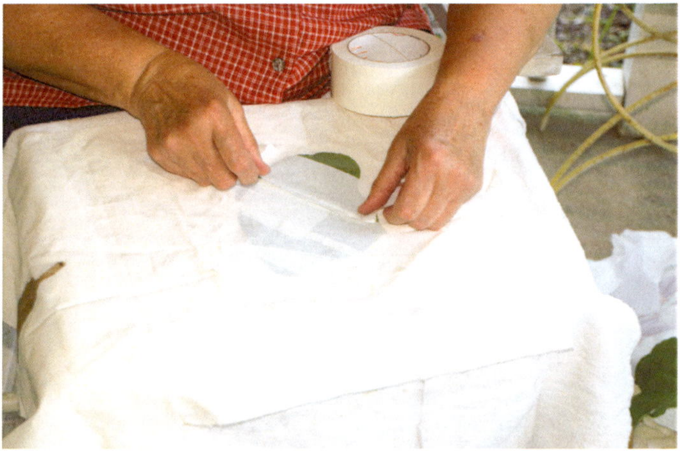

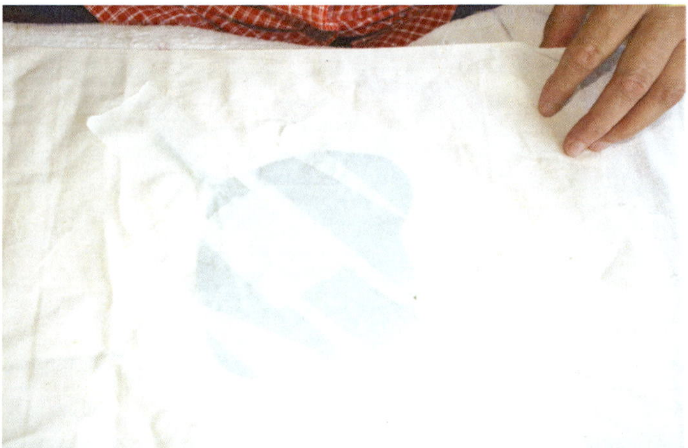

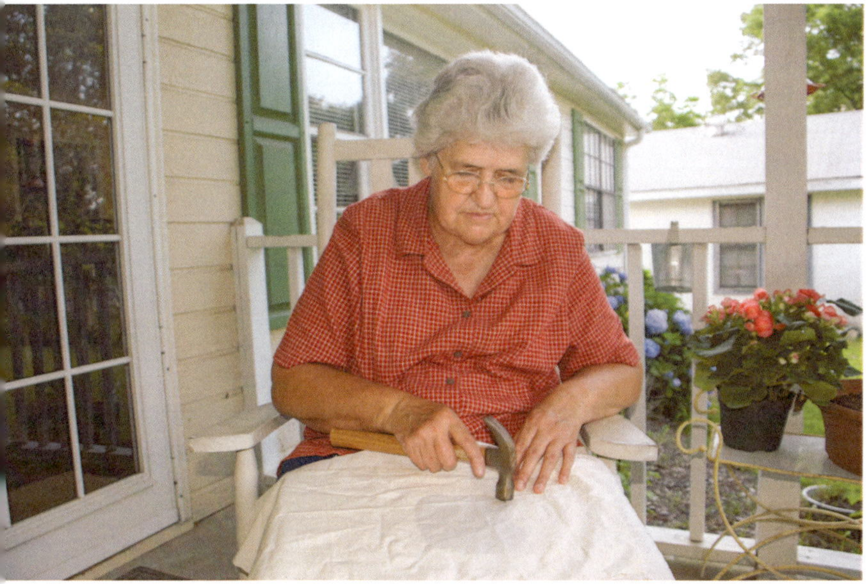

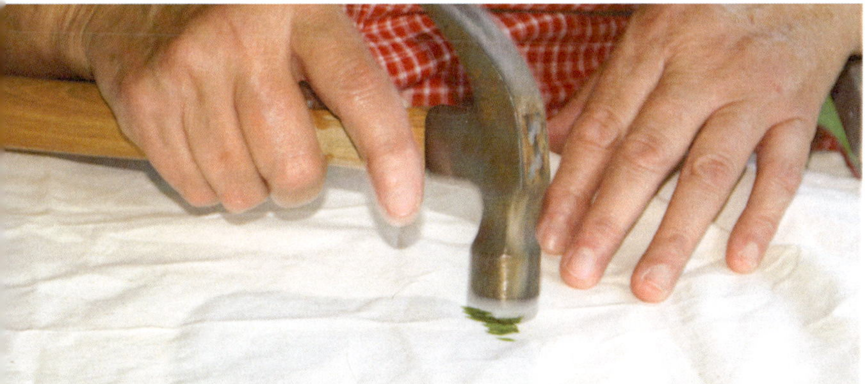

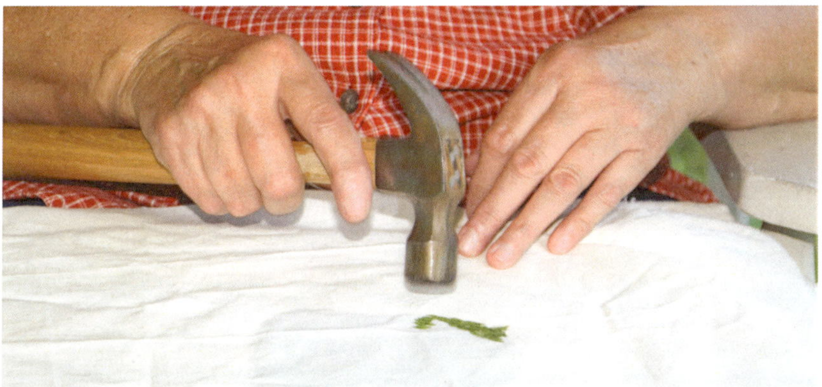

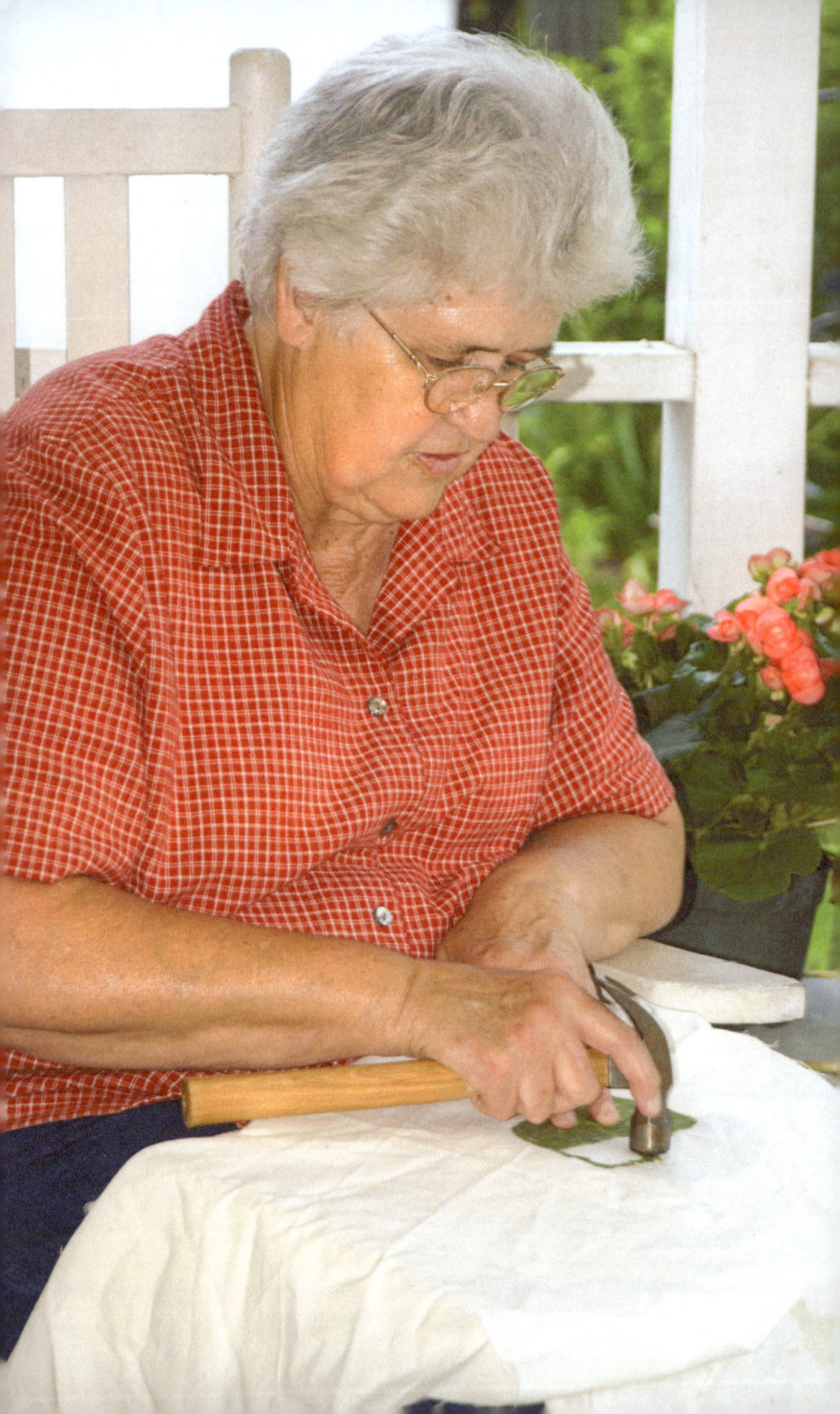

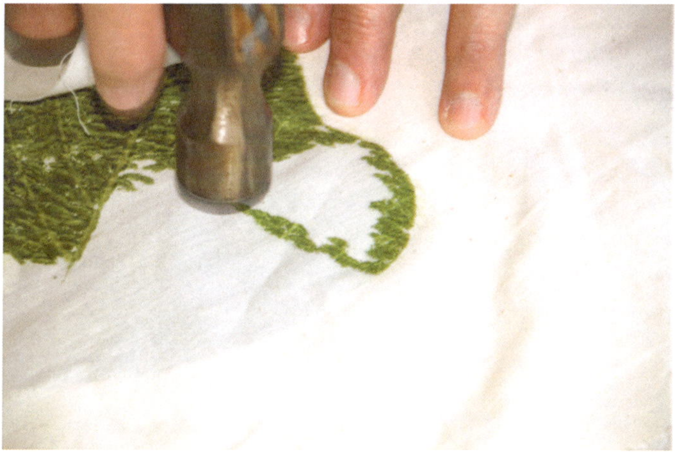

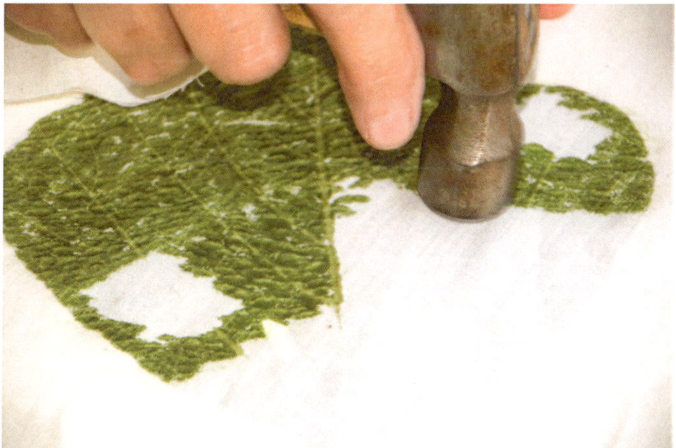

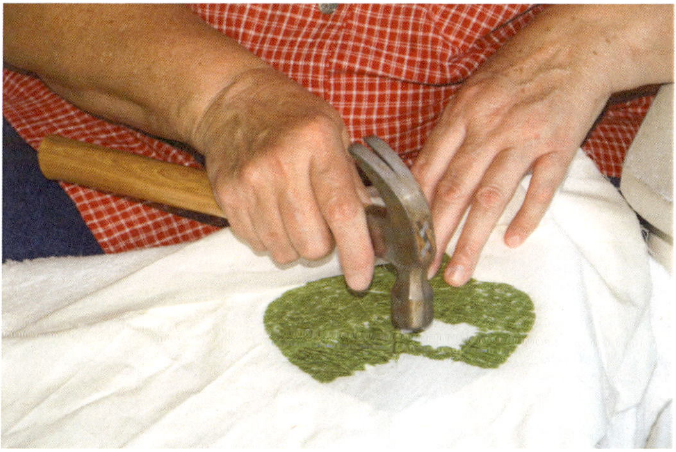

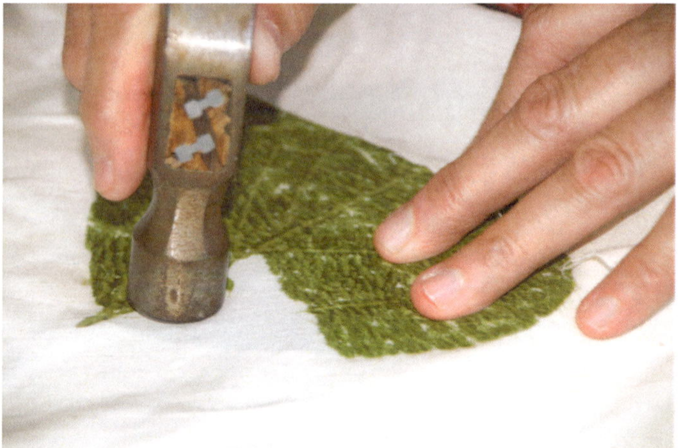

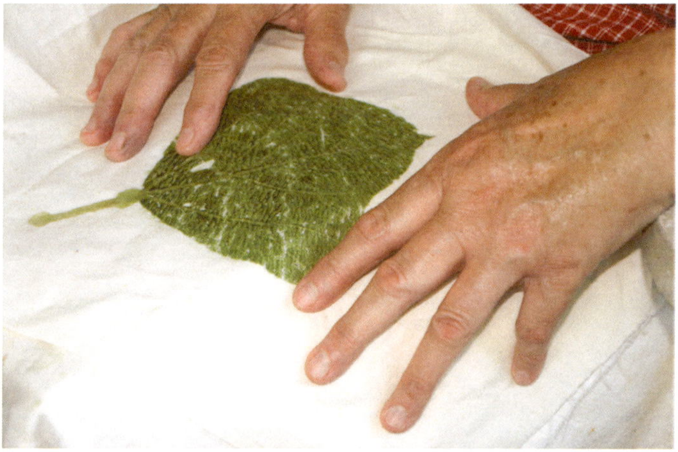

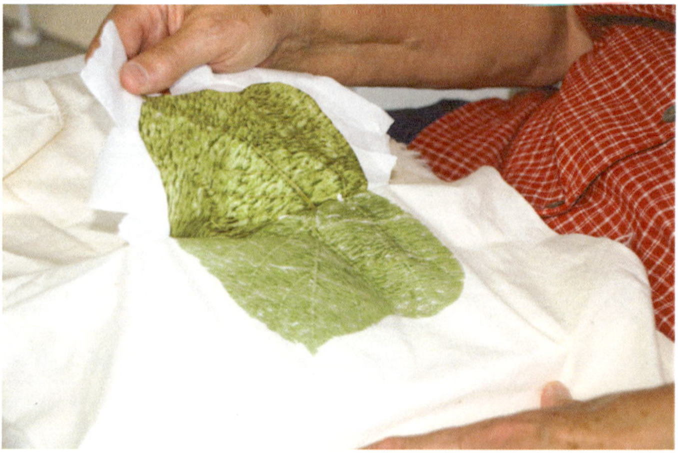

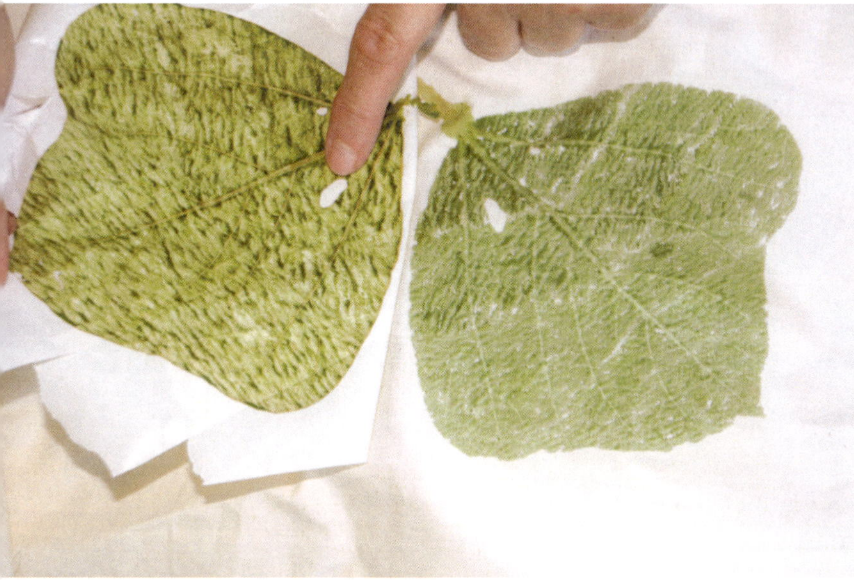

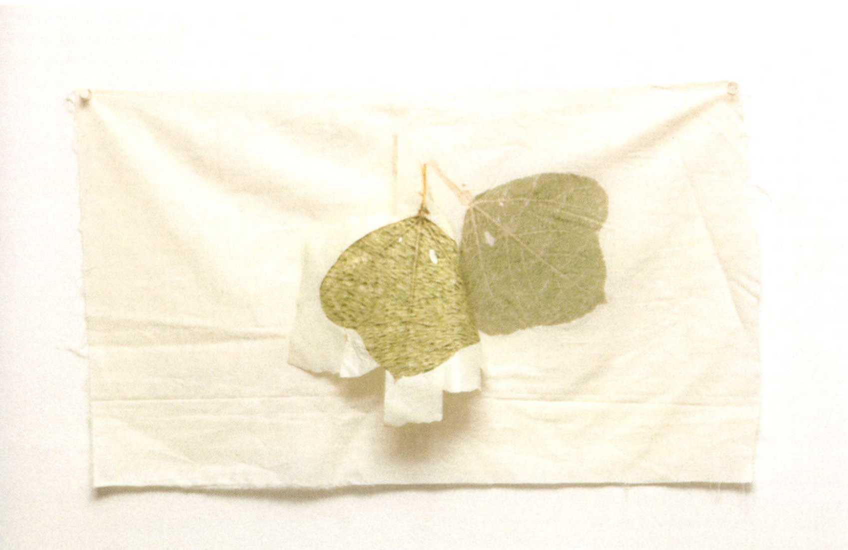

# My Life

I've not been making as many quilts as I should the last couple of years. I think I've been travelling too much and having too much fun because I enjoy the teaching process. If anybody calls me and wants a workshop, a demonstration, as long as I can get to where they are, I go. I never say, "Well, you know, I'm going to charge you $250 in gas," and stuff like this. I never ask them how much they are going to pay me. Because I feel like it's my mission to keep the traditional way of doing these things alive. I'm not a quilt teacher that says, "This is the only way this can be done, and you have to do it this way." I will show them how I do it, and then I say, "Now you take what I've shown you and add your own invention into it and have fun with it."

I ask people to look at a piece of my work, and they say, "It had to take you years to do that." And I tell them, "If you can just work half an hour or an hour a day, you'll be amazed at how quickly you can finish a piece, even though it looks like it took five years. It's just being consistent in doing some of it."

I just want somebody to enjoy it as much as I do and to understand the history behind it, why they did it. When you understand that the old houses were heated by a fireplace and wood stove, they had to have ten quilts on the bed to stay warm.

Quilts are made for every purpose. We have quilts that are made from t-shirts because my son played ball for twelve years and he had fifteen shirts with ball teams on them. We have quilts that are made with ties, because I saved all my husband's ties. We have quilts that are called mourning quilts. I had all these men's shirts left over when my husband passed away, and they were too good to throw away. I turned them into a quilt as a keepsake. Scrap quilts preserve American tradition.

A quilt becomes a special art object to somebody. And for somebody like me that never had that much education and definitely not in the art field, I think God gave all of us a desire to be creative and artistic, and this allows me to do that.

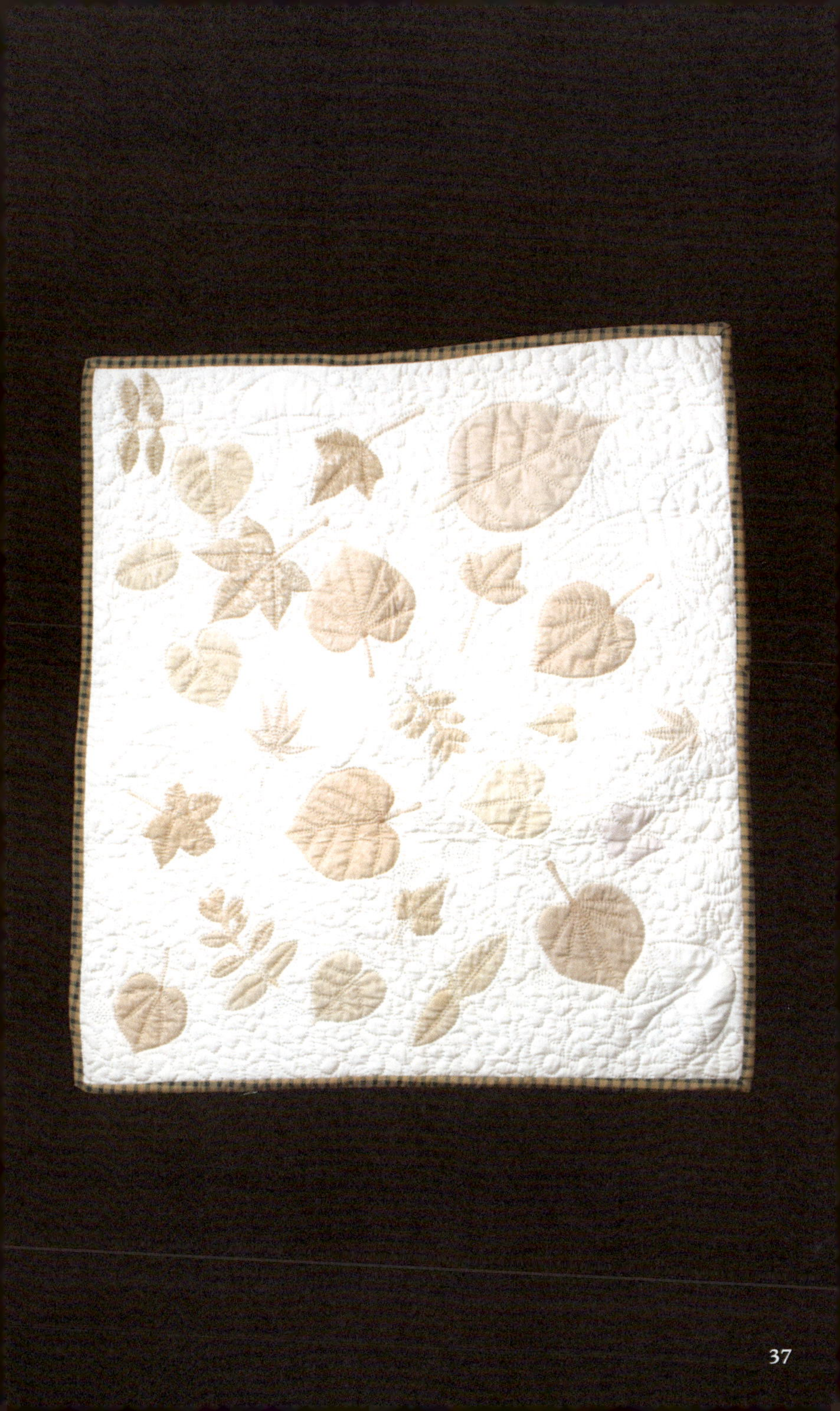

My own children are a wild group. They all have different talents. The girls, all three of them can quilt. Nina is left-handed and she's a little more stubborn, she has to do it her way. Cath is coming along quite well; she's going to be a machine quilter. Cindy pretty much does the design work, and says, "There it is, Mom go for it." I have grandsons that when I'm out at a festival or something, they do the pounding for me. They understand the importance of the quilts, and the quilts all have special family meanings, so they'll be here when I'm gone.

What keeps me going? Oh, goodness. That's a big question. Everything, I think. Just knowing that God has a purpose for me being here and trying to fulfill that purpose. And I think right now with today's society, being a mentor to my grandchildren is my greatest inspiration. My youngest grandson will be eight in August and he's definitely a Meemaw's boy. So, you know, I feel like my children need me. I think I'm needed in my community.

We have such a good group. It's getting out and getting with people. I have a full life in case you hadn't figured that out.

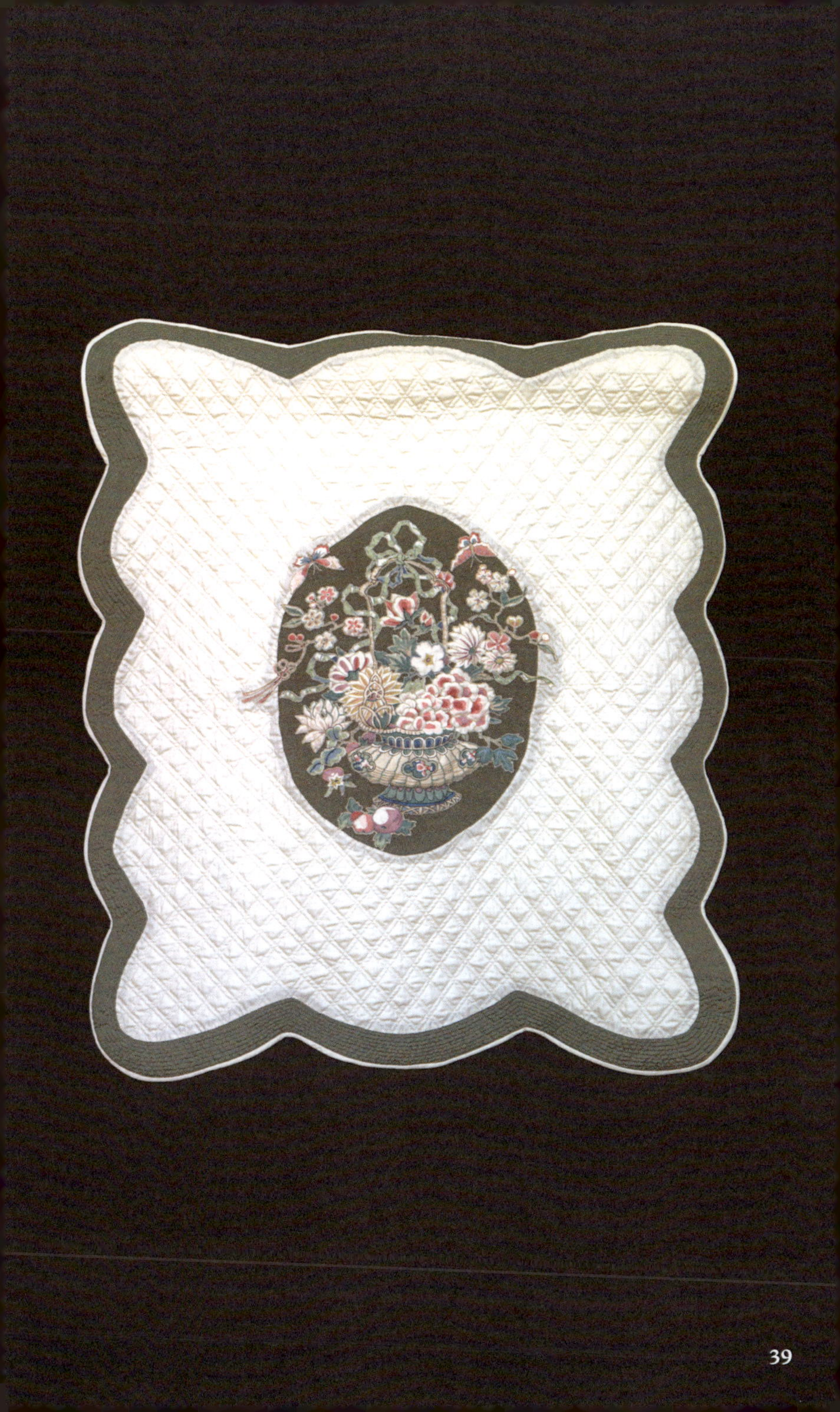

The Bicentennial quilt was an early adaptation of one of Cindy's patterns that I made because my oldest son was in the army for a period of time. My sister had just passed away, and my daughter-in-law thought I needed a project. So, this contest came out in a McCall's magazine and they brought it to me and said, "Well, you got to make this quilt." And it had to be an original design. And, at the time, designing something was beyond my comprehension, but with the group effort of children, contributing ideas and everything, we came up with a fairly decent quilt and it won first place for the state of Alabama.

Basically, it has strip piecing, but it's controlled strips. That means they're cut at a certain size. The stars are appliqued with a buttonhole stitch, which is a little harder to do, but not nearly as hard as trying to turn under the edges of those stars. The eagle block is a pattern that I had gotten as a Christmas gift, and I thought it was right because it represents the presidential medallion. I thought it would go well with the early American flag.

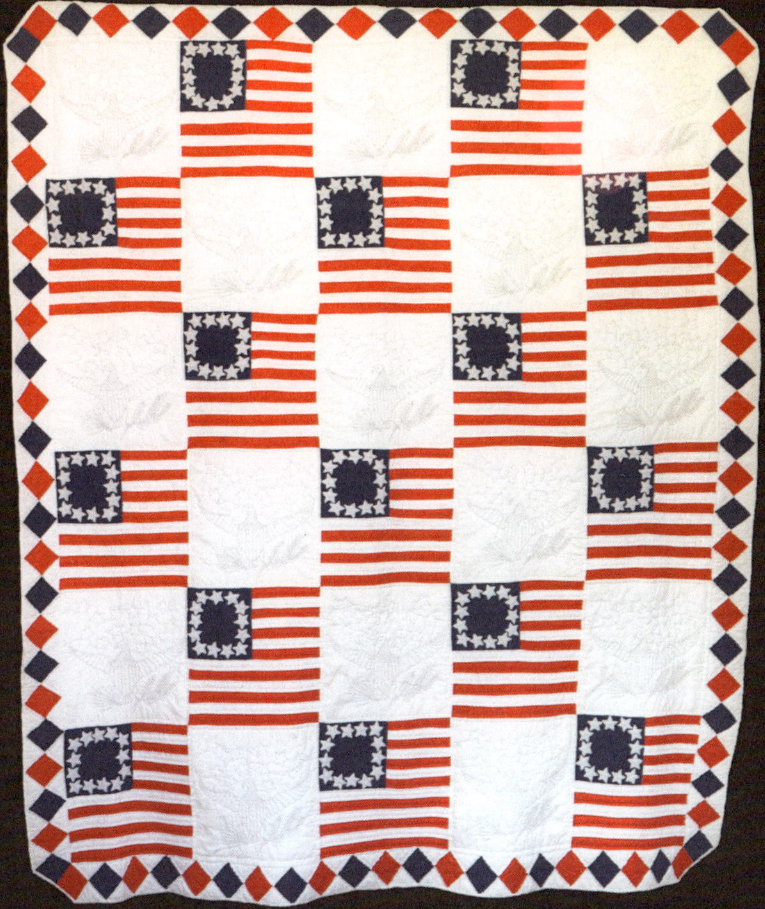

Someone came to the Birmingham Museum and talked about a quilt contest they were going to have for the 200th anniversary of our Constitution. And they asked that for us make a quilt of a certain size with a design that was original. So, I called the girls, all three of them, and said, we need to sit down and design this quilt. And one Sunday afternoon, we sat down and put our ideas together. The grandmother and the wheel in the rocking chair represents my grandmother. In all of Mama's quilts, her block size was a such that twenty blocks would make a quilt. So, the little star quilt that grandmother is quilting on has twenty little stars in it. Kathy, who was an English major, did the wording in there, and Nina, my second daughter developed a real skill with the embroidery needle. And I don't like to embroider, so Nina did all the embroidery work. And Cindy designed the grandmother and helped with the placement of the quilting designs.

The writing in the quilt says, "We, the quilters of the United States of America join this 203rd celebration of our constitution." I can't quote it exactly, but we tried to say we, the quilters, rather than we, the people, so it would have the quilt connotation in it. And, we'd just thought that would say constitution, but also say quilter as well.

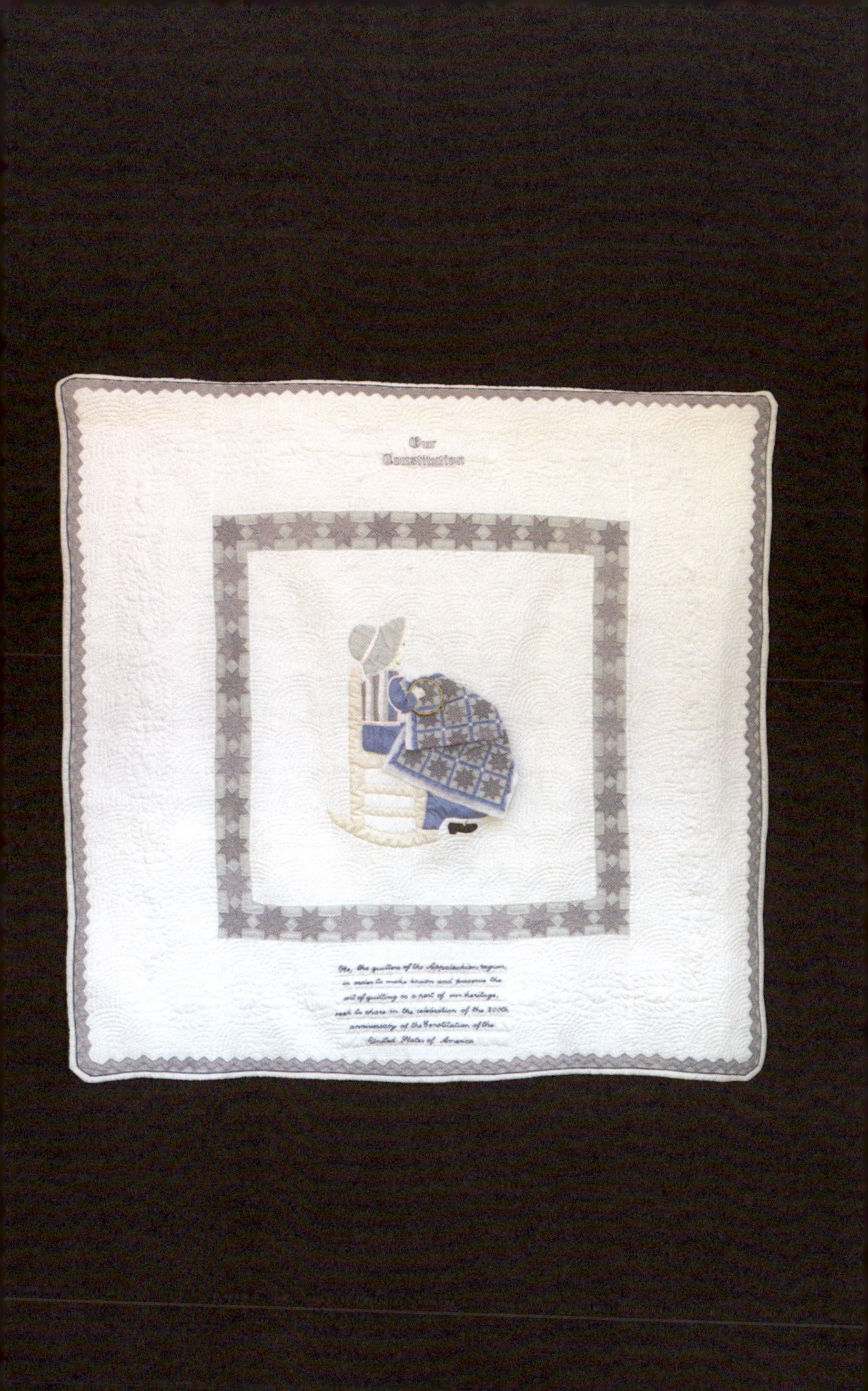
Our Constitution
We, the quilters of the Appalachian region,
in order to make known and preserve the
art of quilting as a part of our heritage,
seek to share in the celebration of the 200th
anniversary of the Constitution of the
United States of America

This table cover goes back to my grandmother's days. She didn't have money to buy really nice things with and she had a table in the living room that they kept the radio on. And, because a feed sack or a fertilizer sack wasn't big enough for the table cover, she would use her crochet needle and create lace and insert lace and make something similar, except she never quilted it. And about fifteen, eighteen year ago, I was thinking about Mama one day and how she created those linens with the insert lace in it and I thought, I bet you, if I really tried, I could do that with a quilt piece. So, that's how that piece came about. The hardest part in that was looking through crochet books and finding a crochet pattern that had the straight edge for the insertion and the scalloped edge for the outside, which I thought added a nice touch to it.

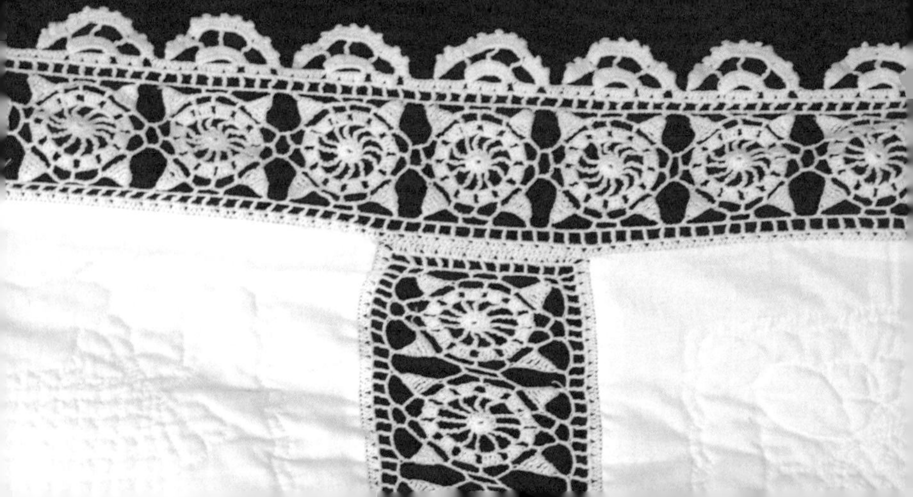

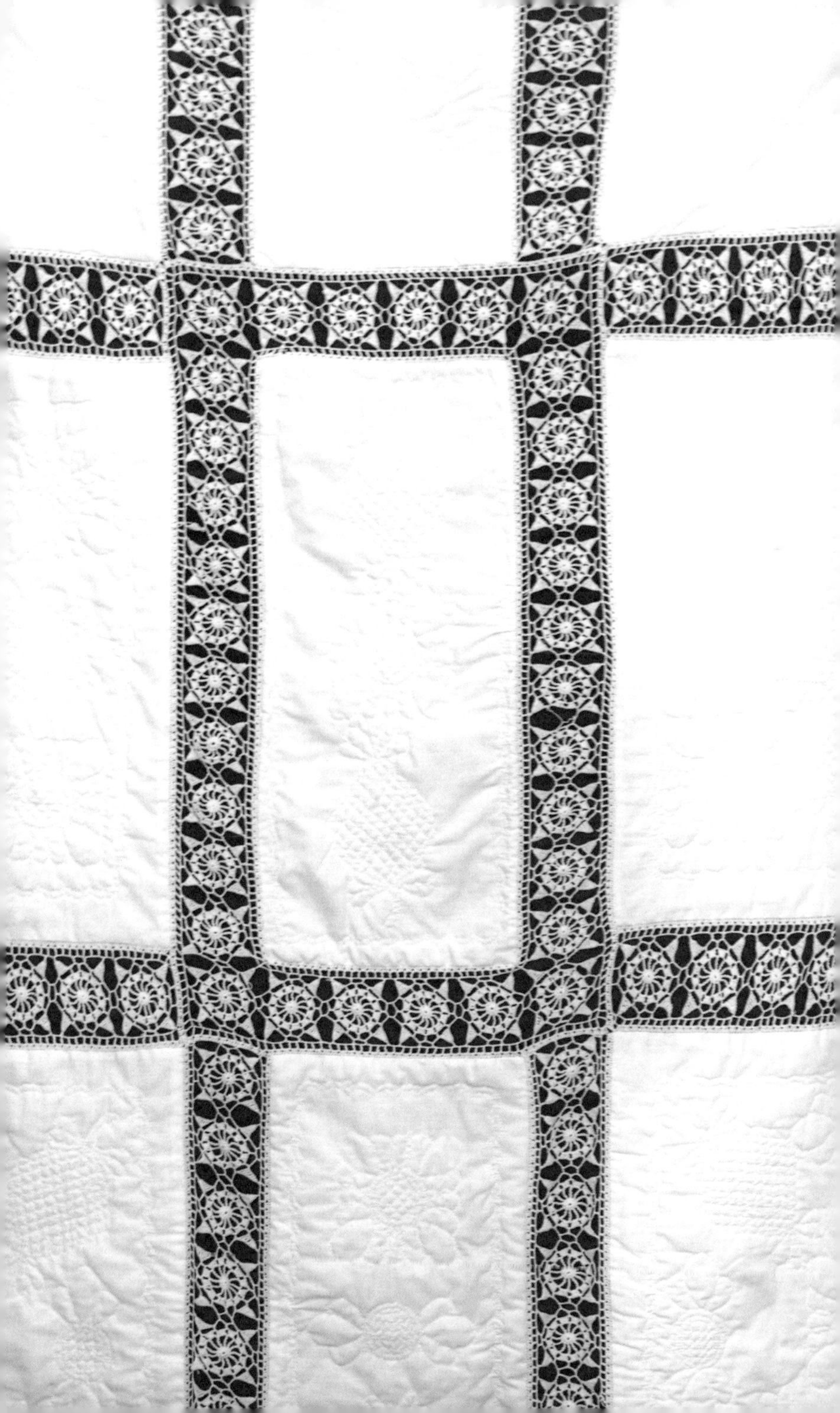

Trapunto is a design that my daughter Cindy drew. She had been to a quilt show with me and she saw Martha's Vineyard, which is a very lovely appliqued quilt. It had hundreds of little dime-sized grapes on it. And she bought the pattern and brought it home and said, "I need you to make this quilt." Well, we pushed that pattern around all over the house and I never did get started on it. And she decided to push me again, and I said, "If you'll sit down and draw that design where I can do it, in trapunto. I will make that quilt for you." So, it's the results of her artwork and mine. Now, we did because, trapunto is an Italian method. And the quilting in the middle is a little bit French because it's called stipple quilting. And their definition of the stipple quilting is quilting as close together as possible without crossing over another stitch, it's pretty much like pointillism in art. And, you're just really adding a lot of texture to the surface.

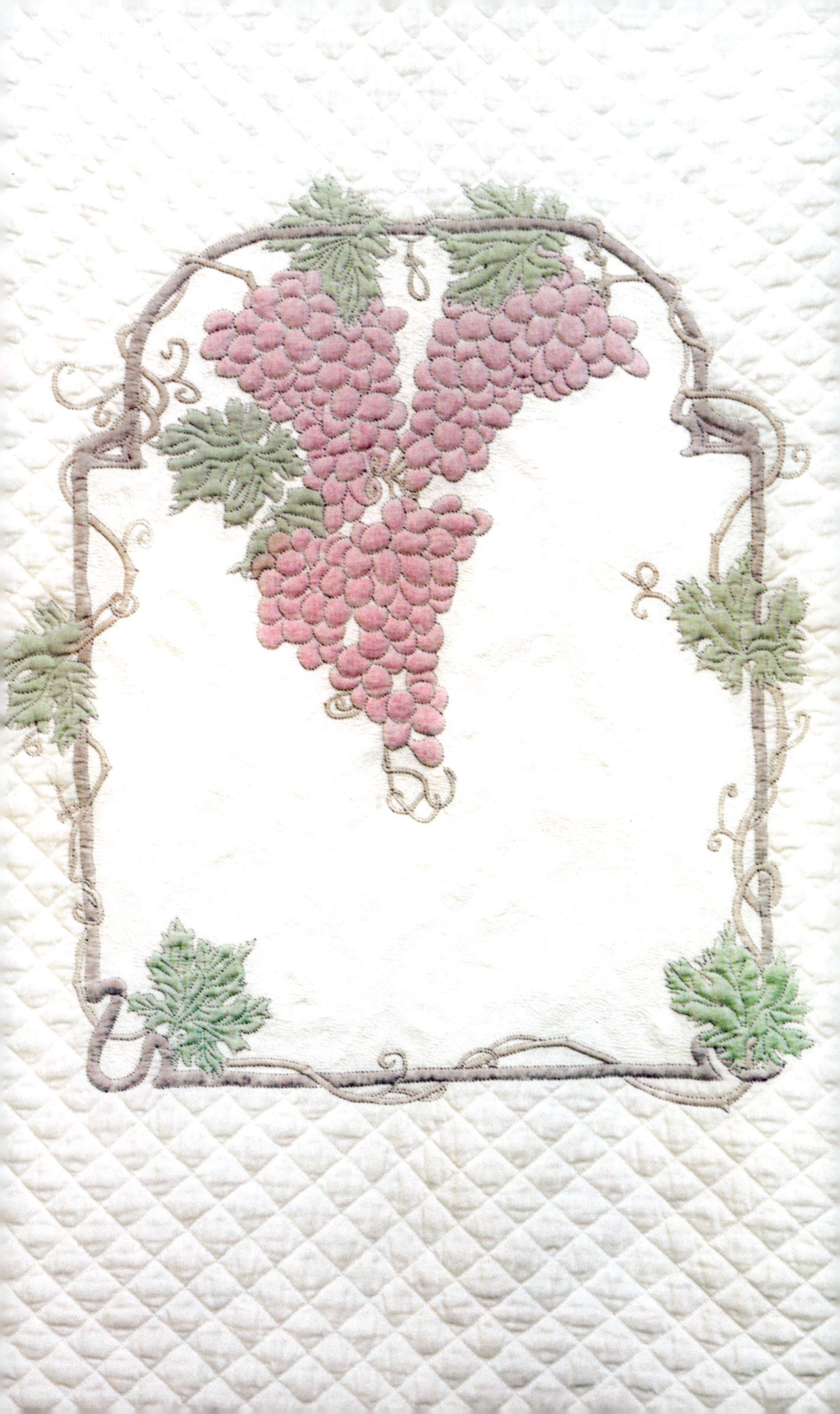

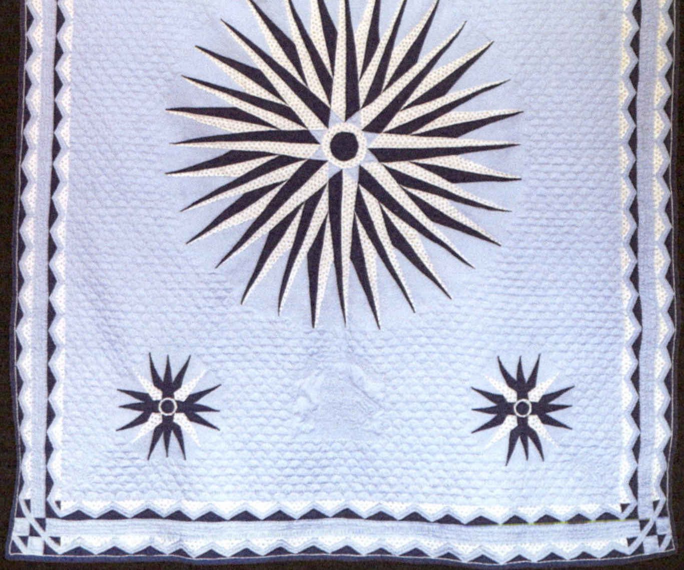

This quilt was made for my son, Scott, as payment for him hauling my quilts to shows. I told him he could pick out any fabric and pattern he wanted. This quilt is called The Mariner's Compass Quilt.

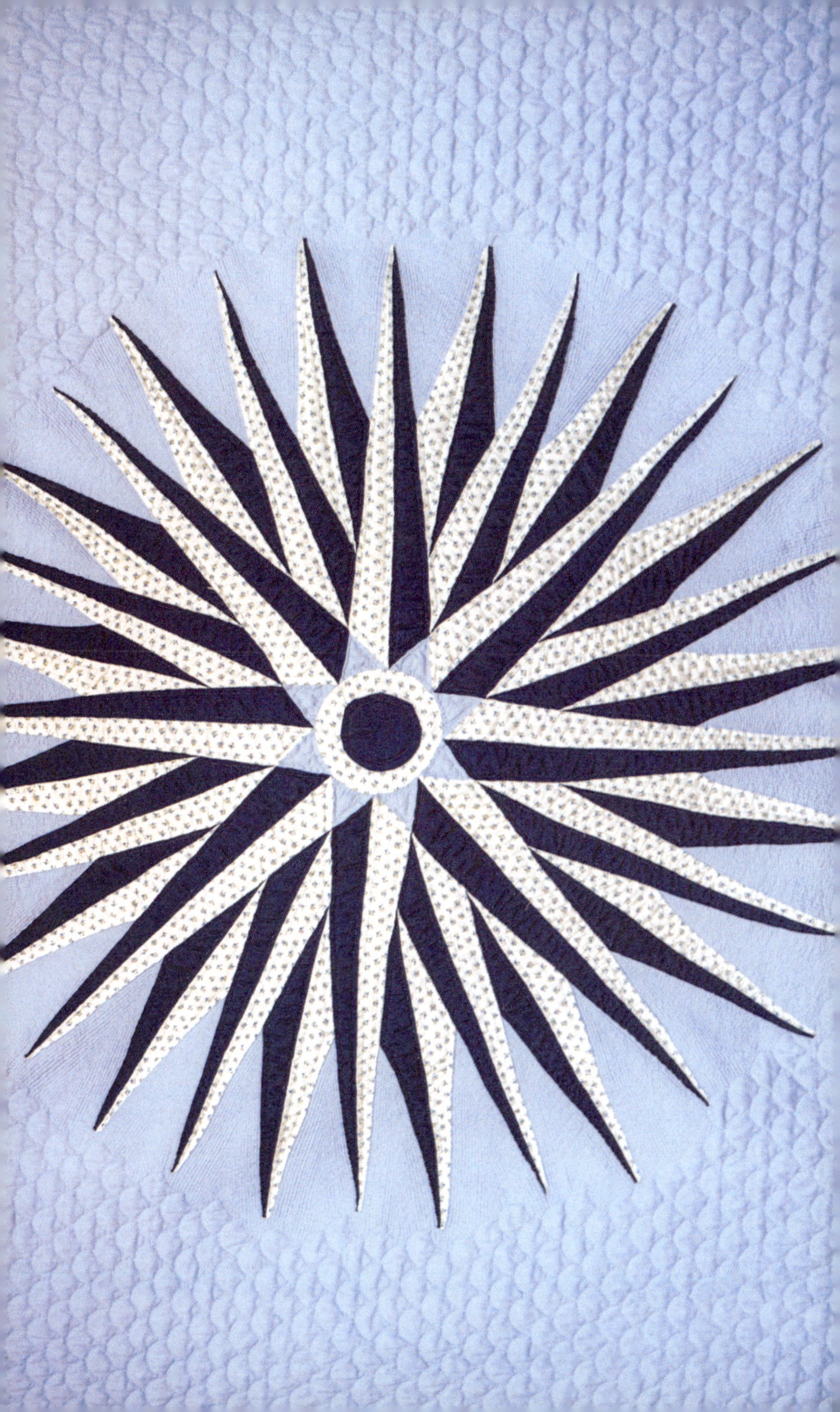

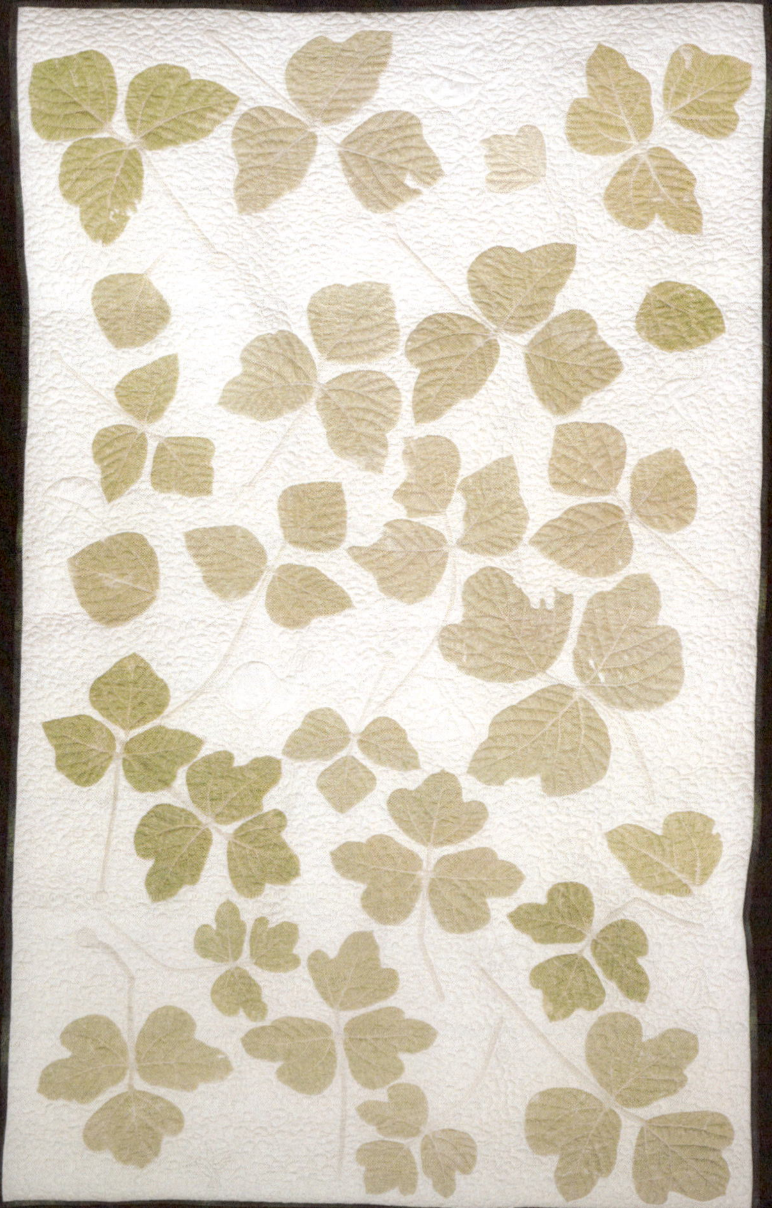

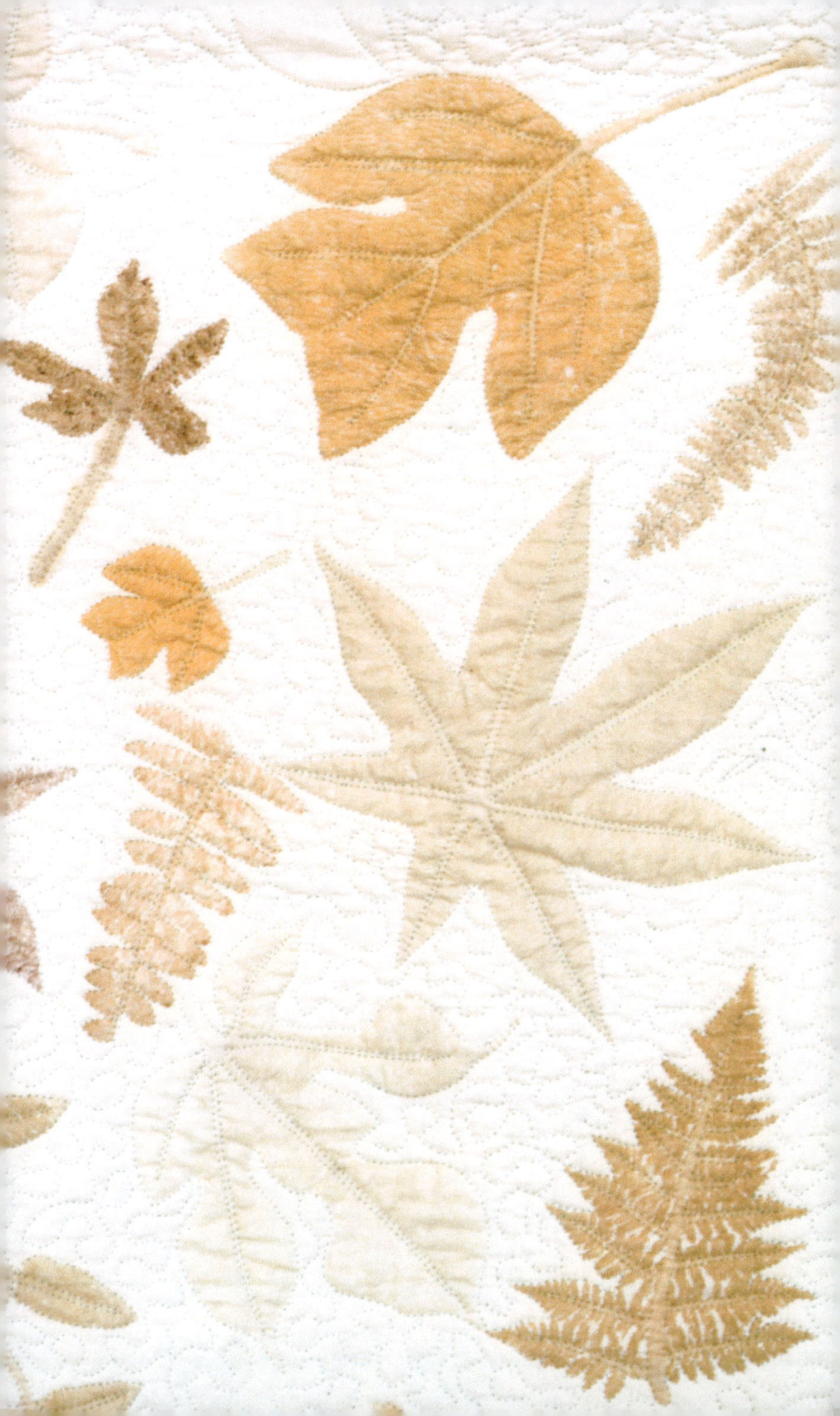

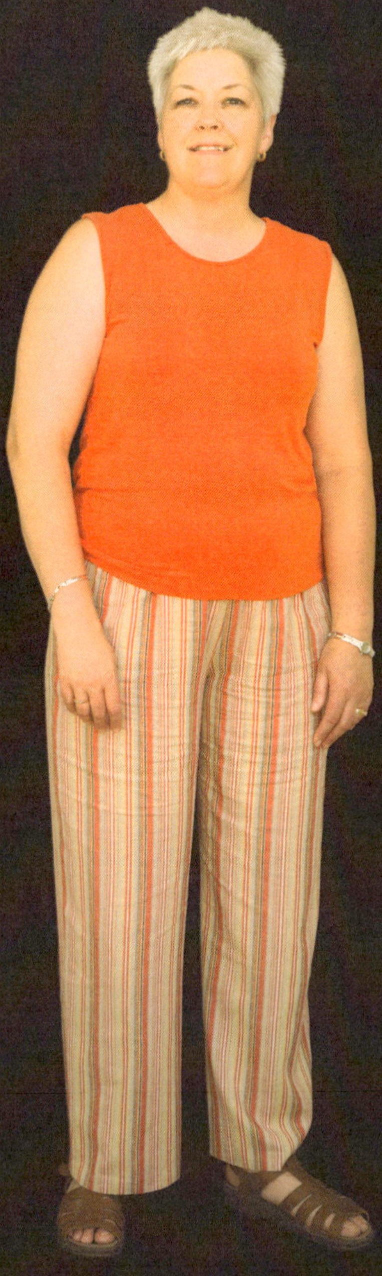

Cindy (Kimbrell) Denton

# Acknowledgements

In making this book, I am grateful to Bettye Kimbrell and her family, who shared her life and artwork, enriching me with her creativity and wisdom.

My wife Kaleta Doolin and my children Alex and Breea often accompanied me on my journeys across the country, offering me their insights and bringing joy to my life.

Over the years, my work on folk and traditional arts was supported in part by grants from the National Endowment for the Arts to Documentary Arts, the non-profit organization I founded in 1985 to advance essential perspectives on historical issues and diverse cultures.

In preparing the manuscript for publication, Anthony Hill and Caitlyn Hood helped to transcribe my interviews, Kevin Todora made studio photographs of artworks, and Jason Johnson-Spinos assisted me in the editing of my texts, processed photographs, and designed the book.

Milton Keynes UK
Ingram Content Group UK Ltd.
UKRC030832021124
450481UK00002B/9

* 9 7 9 8 9 9 1 5 0 2 2 4 5 *